Side by Side

SCHOOL LIBRARY MEDIA SERIES

Edited by Diane de Cordova Biesel

Side by Side

Twelve Multicultural Puppet Plays
for Classroom and Library Production

by
Jean M. Pollock

Original Drawings by Catherine M. Vogt

The Scarecrow Press, Inc.
Lanham, Md., and London
1998

SCARECROW PRESS, INC.

Published in the United States of America
by Scarecrow Press, Inc.
4720 Boston Way
Lanham, Maryland 20706

British Library Cataloguing in Publication Information Available

Library of Congress Cataloging-in-Publication Data

Pollock, Jean M., 1937–
    Side by side : twelve multicultural puppet plays / Jean M.
Pollock.
        p.   cm. — (School library media series ; no. 13)
    Includes bibliographical references (p.   ).
    ISBN 0-8108-3362-X (pbk. : alk. paper)
    1. Puppet plays, American.   2. Fairy tales—Adaptations.
I. Title.   II. Series.
PN1980.P66   1997
791.5'38—dc21   97-20542
                                                  CIP

ISBN 0-8108-3362-X (Pbk. : alk. paper)

For my mother, Margaret Mary Cormier,
in memory of her life of courage and joy

Contents

Foreword

The School Library Media Series is directed to the school library media specialist, particularly the building-level librarian. The multifaceted role of the librarian as educator, collection developer, curriculum developer, and information specialist is examined. The series includes concise, practical books on topical and current subjects related to programs and services.

How do you laugh? Are there little giggles that you cover with your hand? Rythmic chuckles with increasing intensity? Or, do you specialize in audible, open-mouthed guffaws? Any or all of the above will be elicited when you read *Side by Side.* From the wolf dressed as a Girl Scout to the princess-testing bed, Jean Pollock has developed adaptations of traditional stories with wit, style, and flair. Kids will love them. Adults will too.

Diane de Cordova Biesel,
Series Editor

Acknowledgments

Some years ago, my children and I put together a puppet play as part of a birthday celebration. We lit our hand-painted toy stage with candles, dressed animal puppets in costume, and performed a play based on a Japanese folk tale. In writing these plays, I have been able to polish and improve on that memory. For assisting me in this process there are many people to thank.

My colleagues at Los Angeles Public Library (LAPL), Oakland Public Library, and King County Library deserve the greatest thanks for their support, for sharing their expertise and creativity, for encouraging me, and for laughing in all the right places. Children's librarians are among the most resourceful and dedicated professionals in public service today, and I am proud to be one of them. For her trust, vision, and friendship, I thank Jill Jenkins of LAPL. For her willingness to take chances, to perform these plays under truly trying conditions, her insight, her wit, and also her friendship, I am grateful to Kathy Strelioff, also of LAPL. Thanks are also due to Judy Sierra and Bob Kaminski, who shared their expertise with me.

Other colleagues whom I wish to thank are Gay Ducey and Jan Wiggins of Oakland Public Library, and Rosemary Dukelow of Steamboat Springs, Colorado, Public Library. I sincerely thank Ron Stanek of King County Library System (KCLS) for his unfailing kindness. Many thanks also to Dr. Margaret Read MacDonald for her advice and to Miriam, Karen, Avis, and Rebecca. Thank you also to my children—the original puppeteers—and to Maureen for her faith.

I am grateful also to the Blue Lantern Studios for the use of the silhouette images from their collection and to Catherine Vogt, the Mother of Dragons, for her original drawings.

Introduction

When I first became interested in using puppets in library programs, I discovered that there were few interesting scripts suitable for amateur puppeteers or appropriate for performance in library and school settings. I decided to write my plays taking into account the puppet collection available to me, the time available for rehearsal and performance, the number of puppeteers, and my small abilities as a puppeteer. I made a few puppets and borrowed some others, enlisted the help of another children's librarian with the promise that the play would be performed at her branch as well as mine, and began writing. In my ten years as a children's librarian, I have performed these plays many times. Several children's librarians from Los Angeles Public Library have performed them without my assistance and found them to be successful and feasible for even the less daring librarians and teachers.

I have also directed several puppetry workshops with children. The children used my puppets and also made some of their own. We made hand puppets, shadow puppets, and stick puppets. Besides performing plays, their puppets sang songs, recited poems, and acted as "masters of ceremony." Based on these workshop experiences, I believe that classroom use of these plays would be fun and instructive. The scripts and the folk tales from which they are taken are a natural and thoroughly enjoyable way to enrich curricula and incorporate a whole language approach.

This collection acknowledges that children know what is funny and what is not, appreciate and use witticisms, and have the sophistication to follow a plot and participate in the joy of creating an illusion. Playful and fast paced, the scripts are not insulting to the verbal abilities of bright young performers and audiences. They are all based on folk tales and fairy tales. Most are well-known stories, and all are simple enough to be suitable for young audiences. The humor and interaction between puppets and the audience will extend the appeal to older children as well. Also, children in grade four and up will find performing the plays for younger audiences to be challenging. The familiar and simple story lines enable young performers to focus on technique and work toward a smooth and creditable production.

There are many fine books on using puppets with children (see General Bibliography). Many focus on puppetry as a type of dramatic play and emphasize the process of making puppets, often from found materials. Scripts are then created to suit the puppet characters. These books are full of delightfully inventive and instructive ideas and should be the basis for any work with children and puppets. This collection, however, will help take interested children to the next step of performing a scripted play for an audience of families and classmates.

Getting Started

Puppets

You may choose to make your puppets, have them made, or buy commercial puppets. It was through a combination of all three methods that I acquired my collection. Let it be known that you are interested in building a classroom or library puppet collection, and puppets will happen. Your school or library may have funds to spend on puppets. Local businesses too small to make grand gestures might be willing to sponsor a puppet. Creative patrons or parents might enjoy making a puppet or two. Approach community organizations with small and medium budgets for help in building your collection. Projects that are easily accomplished and do not involve a large expenditure of time or money often appeal to these organizations.

People puppets are more problematic than animal puppets, which are more readily available and/or easier to make. The material I found

easiest to use is instant papier-mâché over Styrofoam eggs. This makes a good basic head shape that is light but sturdy. If you have money to spend, I would suggest buying or having someone make people puppets. The people puppets used in a play should be consistent with each other in style and material. A collection should include a young couple, an older couple, and a girl and boy. This assortment will cover most needs.

Witches, monsters, fairies, etc. need not be consistent with the people puppets and could even be animal puppets in costume. Animal puppets can be dressed as humans in wigs and costumes for minor roles. The entire cast can be composed of costumed, wigged animal puppets. If you want to make your own puppets, the General Bibliography includes books of patterns. Often patterns for dolls and stuffed animals can be adjusted to work as hand puppets. Stuffed toy animals can sometimes be turned into animal hand puppets. Experiment with different materials. One of the cleverest puppets I have ever seen was made out of a string mop head.

Try contacting high school and community college art departments to find out if there are any talented young student artists interested in trying their hands at the craft of puppet making. I know of a high school student in Los Angeles who made a cast of people puppets and gave them to a branch of LAPL as a community service project. Local or state puppetry guilds can also give you the names and addresses of professional puppet makers in your area.

If you want to use the scripts but the problems of using puppets seem insurmountable, use masks instead. A very different performance will result, but it too can be charming and fun.

Puppet Movement

In the classroom you will want to plan a training period for your puppeteers using short skits, improvisation, songs, poems, and short readings. Allow the entire group access to all the puppets for a time to see which students emerge as enthusiastic puppeteers. Experiment with different movements such as walking, running, lying down, sitting down, bowing, pointing, talking to another character, and talking to the audience. Encourage your puppeteers to practice movement in front of a mirror. They will soon discover that bobbing a puppet up and down is not as effective as a slight side-to-side movement. They will also find that puppets must look somewhere—at the audience, at each other, or at a prop. If a script directs the puppet to speak to the audience, the puppet must lean out over the edge of the stage and direct the words at the audience so that the effect of involvement is adequately stressed.

Puppets must face the direction in which they are moving unless a comic effect is desired. Speed and style of movement can indicate that the puppet is frightened or confident, excited or stuffy, happy or sad. Try different paces for puppet movement. Practice the movement until it feels natural and a part of the speech that the puppet is making. Be sure that whatever the puppet is doing is being done well above stage level so that members of the audience who are up front will not have their view of the action blocked by the edge of the stage.

Puppeteers should wear black sleeves or gloves so that their wrists and forearms will not show. Holding a puppet above your head for fifteen minutes is very tiring. Holding two puppets above your head is very, very tiring. Children should use only one puppet at a time so that they can support their elbows with their other hand. Encourage puppeteers to rest their arms at every opportunity.

Voice

Amateur puppeteers should use a natural voice unless they are very, very confident. Paying attention to the emotional state of a particular puppet character will result in a more convincing delivery than will attempting to adopt a completely different voice for each puppet and each situation. With the puppet's character well in mind, slight changes in pitch, volume, and pace will be enough to distinguish one character from another. Puppets should move when they speak, and the other puppets should be still and silent. If student puppeteers are tempted to rush their lines, remind them that their audience will include many small children—so they must speak slowly. This applies to librarian puppeteers as well.

Scripts and Lines

Highlight each character's lines on the scripts with a different color for each character. Underline the stage directions so they will not be confused with the highlighted speeches. You must decide if your puppeteers will memorize their scripts or read them. Some puppet experts feel strongly that scripts should be memorized to truly participate in and experience the art of puppet drama. I have never attempted to memorize a script; the time available for putting together library programs would never permit it. However, in a classroom situation, a teacher might find it easier than manipulating a number of script pages. I pin or tape the pages of the scripts to the back of the puppet theater. Two copies of the script are usually needed so that all the puppeteers have their lines directly in front of them. Number the pages in very large figures so that puppeteers can find their place easily.

Puppet Stages

Stages can be bought or improvised. Puppetry guilds can give you the names and addresses of puppet stage suppliers. However, putting a stage together is simpler than making puppets. For your first effort, put two chairs on a low table, lay a broom handle across their backs, and cover it all with a curtain. Put a table on its side and drape it with a sheet for another instant theater. As you experiment, you will discover what features your puppet stage must have. Mobility was important to me. I needed a stage that could be broken down into sections and put into a small car to take to another library.

The basic puppet stage is a frame made of metal, wood, or PVC pipe from which curtains are hung to hide the puppeteers. There must be a way to hang or attach a backdrop behind the stage. A small shelf three or four inches wide and running the length of the playing area is useful for placing props. However, the props can be made so that they can be pinned or taped to the stage curtain if you do not have a shelf. The bottom of the stage must be weighted or made of heavy material so that the stage is not knocked over. Having your stage fall over is a disaster from which it is difficult to recover. The type of stage that is made of three panels hinged together with a window cut out in the central panel is the least useful for a large number of puppeteers and for the plays in this book.

Sets and Props

Use the entire puppet stage to create your illusion. As you gain confidence, experiment with testing the limits of the playing area. Extend your action and decoration beyond the limits of the stage. Thrust the puppets through breaks in the front curtains, above backdrops, and around the edge of the stage. Carry a puppet into the audience to talk in character with the children. Include interaction between people and puppets as part of the illusion.

Attach two-dimensional set pieces to the curtains at the front of the stage. Attach cutout letters spelling the title of the play to the front curtains. For a castle scene paint cobblestones on a piece of cloth and drape it over the front of the stage. Use paisley prints for rugs. I have seen a puppeteer use several stages and move the puppets between them in full view of the audience. Sets should not obstruct the view or movement of the puppets. Keep them minimal, only suggesting a house, a forest, a castle, etc.

Props are difficult for amateur puppeteers to handle. Make sure they are big enough to be seen and recognized, and light enough to manipulate. Practice handling props thoroughly. Practice dropping props and getting them back with the help of a backstage assistant or even a member of the audience.

Backstage

The arrangement of the backstage area is very important whether the puppeteers are adults or children. Positioning puppeteers, taking puppets on and off, and deciding where to position puppeteer assistants and sound effects persons should be worked out in an early rehearsal and noted on a chart. Props and puppets should be placed on a table in the order in which they are to be used, and that arrangement should be recorded on a chart. Store props and puppets in a box under the table when they are no longer needed. If later rehearsals reveal a problem that was not anticipated, make the change and rehearse it into the performance. Backstage traffic management when children are the puppeteers should be carefully worked out ahead of time with all scripts annotated to record details. Children should leave the playing area quickly and quietly when their turn is over. Remind the children of the need for quiet and order backstage, but make sure they are having fun too.

Quality Checks

Ask a colleague or helper who is somewhat detail oriented to observe a rehearsal midway through the schedule and, if possible, near the end. Ask this person to sit in different places in the room while they watch a rehearsal and make notes of any problems they observe. Can the puppets be seen easily? Can they be heard and understood? Is anything in the action or script confusing or unconvincing?

Support Material

Following each play you will find information on the production and use of that play. The arrangement of this support material is as follows:

Playing Notes

Puppets and Puppeteers

Classroom Production: Numbers and types of puppets and puppeteers needed and ways to involve an entire class.

Library Production: Limit number of puppets and puppeteers and ways to simplify for a quick production.

Props and Scenery

Specific suggestions and how to make them.

Action

Descriptions of the traits and styles of characters in the play with suggestions on how to achieve certain effects.

Program Building

Library Programs: Suggestions of books, stories, music, and short crafts to create a thirty- to forty-minute program

Classroom Study Units: Explain ways in which the play can be used as the focus of a unit on subjects such as astronomy, Native Americans, animal studies, geography, history, etc.

Bibliography

Each play has its own bibliography listing titles of books and media that can be used to develop a study unit or program around that play. The titles are grouped into Picture Books, Longer Fiction, Nonfiction, and Media. In some, the Nonfiction group is further divided into subject areas such as biographies, Native American studies, cookbooks, poetry, etc.

Also Helpful

Appendix

Each of the plays is suitable for classroom or library production. However, library production assumes a limited number of puppeteers and backstage help as well as a shorter time for preparation. The support material for each play suggests ways to change the script to make it suitable for a cast of two puppeteers and a helper. For some plays the changes are so extensive as to require a separate script. The abbreviated scripts will be found in this appendix.

General Bibliography

In this section you will find lists of books on puppets and puppetry for children and adults, storytelling, and children's literature. Videos and compact discs are also included in this list.

Not to Forget

Remind yourself to have fun. Playfulness will spread and provide cover as you and your students gain skill and confidence. During one of my early productions of *The Princess and the Pea*, the bed was made of several mattresses with strips of Velcro glued to them. Giles, the servant puppet, brought each mattress in, singly, and slapped it with great gusto onto the preceding one. After about six mattresses were in place, he slapped on the next one with a little too much gusto (probably because he had to reach up very high by this time). The entire stack of mattresses burst apart and was sent flying out into the audience. There were screams of laughter, then children picked up the mattresses and brought them up to the stage where we reached out and got them. Giles thanked them profusely and we continued with a bed put together backstage. I have redesigned the bed, not wishing to repeat this experience. The instructions for the new and improved model are with the script for *The Princess and the Pea*. Be prepared to welcome a great deal of playfulness and silliness in the creation of puppet drama. Make any changes in the scripts that please you and enjoy!

1

The Animals' Tug-of-War

Performers: grades 4 through 6
Audience: preschool through grade 3
Cast: Whale
      Elephant
      Rabbit
      Turtle
      Cheering Section

Props: Rope; two buckets of confetti, one blue, green, and white, one green and brown.

Set: Water on stage left, grass on stage right, and a tree in the middle. A green backdrop at rear. Two feet upstage, a blue backdrop.

Whale rises up at stage left and sputters. Rabbit pops up at center stage and moves to stage left.

Rabbit: Whale, oh Whale, would you like to play? Maybe a jumping contest.

Whale: Sputter *Bit of confetti flies up.* What was that Rabbit? You want to play with me? You want to have a jumping contest with me, a mighty denizen of the deep? Ha, ha, ha! *Flips over and waggles his tail in the air, then turns up again.* Hee, hee, hee! Me in a jumping contest with you. Rabbit, I can jump as high as two hundred rabbits,

7

and when I fall back into the water, I make a splash as big as your island. Oh Rabbity Rabbit, you are so little that if you fell into the water you would not even make a ripple.

Rabbit: Well, I was just trying to be neighborly! Humph. I'll just find someone else to talk to who has better manners. *Turns.* Thinks he's such a smarty pants-big fish-big blowhard. What does bigness matter anyway? *Goes to stage right, grumbling and mumbling all the way and approaches elephant.*

Rabbit: Hi there, Elephant.

Elephant: What? Who's that saying hello to me? *looks about*

Rabbit: It's me. Down here, Elephant! It's me—Rabbit. Want to play something?

Elephant: You must be joking. Me play with you? Me, a powerful but pleasant pachyderm, play with you, a bunny rabbit? Ho, ho, ho. Now go away bunny before I pick you up in my trunk and throw you to the other side of the world.

Rabbit: You know, Mr. Elephant, size isn't everything. Manners count for something.

Elephant: Oh go away! *turns his back on Rabbit*

Rabbit: on way to center stage That Elephant! He's as bad as Whale.

Turtle: enters from below center stage What are you grumbling about, Rabbit? Are you still mad about that race we had? I was just trying to teach you a lesson.

Rabbit: Hi Turtle. What race? You and I had a race? I don't remember that. Besides, anyone can have a bad day. I just asked Whale to play with me, and he said no, that I was too small. Then I asked Elephant, and she said no too. Both of them made very rude remarks about small people like you and me. Do we have to put up with this disrespect, Turtle? I'm very quick and clever, and you have that trick you do where you pull your head and feet inside your shell. That's spectacular, Turtle.

Turtle: It is rather spectacular, isn't it? But, Rabbit, it doesn't do any good to complain about it. Whale and Elephant will just laugh at us more. We must show them that small animals are not silly and helpless.

Rabbit: I'm just going to march up to that Elephant and punch her right in that big nose of hers. And after that I'm going to grab Whale by the tail and swing him around and around and then let him go—right up to the moon!

SCHOOL LIBRARY MEDIA SERIES

Edited by Diane de Cordova Biesel

Side by Side

Turtle: Now, now, Rabbit. You know that won't work. They really are a lot bigger than you. We must trick them! It's the only way.

Rabbit: I know! Let's trick them into fighting with each other. I'll tell Whale that Elephant said he is a really ugly creature, more like a fish than a mammal. Then I'll tell Elephant that Whale said her trunk was the silliest nose in the animal kingdom. Then they'll fight, and then . . .

Turtle: Calm down, Rabbit! *Pats Rabbit on the shoulder.* There. Now, we must think.

Rabbit: Okay. Think! Think! Think! Think! *Taps head.*

Turtle: Let's see. Whale lives in the water.

Rabbit: Right.

Turtle: Elephant lives on the plain.

Rabbit: Right.

Turtle: We must find something that links them.

Rabbit: How about a rope? A strong rope could link them together.

Turtle: Oh Rabbit. I didn't mean really link them. I meant . . . Hey, wait a minute. I think you just gave me an idea.

Rabbit: I did? What was my idea Turtle?

Turtle: A rope to link them together. They could have a tug-of-war. But, but, they won't know it. You will make each one of them think that they are having a tug-of-war with you. Only, instead of having a tug-of-war with you, they will be having a tug-of-war with each other!

Rabbit: Let me see. Whale will think he is having a tug-of-war with me, and Elephant will think she is having a tug-of-war with me too, right?

Turtle: Yes. Either Whale or Elephant could win a tug-of-war with you. And easily, I might add.

Rabbit: But, they won't be having a tug-of-war with me at all. They will be having a tug-of-war with each other. And it will be very difficult for either one to win. Great! But how?

Turtle: Let me see. Aha! The water is way over there. *Gestures.* And the plain is way over there. *Gestures and Rabbit looks both ways.* See the tree between them. If we had a really long rope . . . Yes!

Rabbit: I'll get the rope. *Exits below center stage and returns with rope.* Here. Now what?

Turtle: Take this end of the rope and go challenge Whale to a tug-of-war.

Rabbit: O.K. *Goes to stage left.* Oh mighty Whale, I have thought of a game for us to play. Do you want to play Tug-of-war?

Whale: Ha! Small, little Rabbit, I am twenty million trillion times stronger than you.

Rabbit: Maybe. Or maybe you just think you are stronger. Wouldn't you like to prove it? Perhaps you are afraid.

Whale: Afraid?! Just give me that rope!

Rabbit: *Puts rope in Whale's mouth.* All right! Now don't pull until I yell "ready." And if I win, you must agree that I am your equal.

Whale: Fine.

Rabbit: returns to Turtle at center stage carrying other end of rope Now for Elephant.

Turtle: Go Rabbit!

Rabbit: goes to stage right with rope Oh Elephant? You think you are stronger than I am, don't you?

Elephant: Humph. I know I am, oh tiny and insignificant speck of fur.

Rabbit: Well, if I could beat you in a tug-of-war, would you agree that I am your equal?

Elephant: Ha, ha, ha, ha ha. Oh Rabbit, you are funny. A most humorous hare. Sure. Why not. I don't have anything else to do today.

Rabbit: Here's the rope, Elephant. Now don't pull until I yell "ready."

Elephant: What a bore! Yes, Rabbit, yes.

Rabbit: returns to Turtle at center stage Elephant and Whale each have an end of the rope. Should I yell "ready"?

Turtle: Not yet. First we must have a cheering section. Hey everyone!

Animals of cheering section rise up between the green and blue backdrop.

Animals: Yes?

Turtle: Will you cheer for Rabbit?

Animals: Sure. Of course. Anytime. Tell us when you're ready.

Turtle: Now we must ask those boys and girls out there to help us.

Rabbit: What boys and girls? O! *Cry of fear.* I didn't see them.

Turtle: It's OK, Rabbit. They're friendly. Aren't you? *Audience reacts.*

Turtle: Hey, boys and girls. You must help us convince these two bullies that they are having a tug-of-war with Rabbit. So I want you to yell and cheer for Rabbit, okay? Good. We'll practice. Yell "Pull Rabbit pull!" Louder! Great. Now yell "Rabbit is winning, Rabbit is winning!" Very good. Now yell "Way to go Rabbit, way to go!" Fantastic. Now chant "Ra-bbit, Ra-bbit, Ra-bbit, Ra-bbit." Wonderful! During the tug-of-war you must keep yelling and cheering. Rabbit, you must grunt and growl. *rabbit nods* Now yell "ready!"

Rabbit: Spells R-E-A-D-Y Ready!

Turtle: Leads audience and animals in cheering Rabbit. Pull, Rabbit, pull! Way to go Rabbit! Ra-bbit, Ra-bbit, Ra-bbit! Rabbit is winning, Rabbit is winning! *Repeats these as long as tug-of-war lasts.*

Whale and Elephant pull on the rope with much grunting, groaning, and growling. The blue, white, and green paper balls are tossed over the top of the stage and into the audience from the Whale's side of the stage. The same thing happens on the Elephant's side with the green and brown paper balls. The tug-of-war lasts as long as the paper balls and the puppeteer's strength hold out. Rabbit dashes from one side of the tree to the other grunting, groaning, and yelling but never leaves center stage. At the same moment, Whale and Elephant let go and fall back, each with a groan, behind the stage and out of view.

Rabbit: Goes to stage left. Who won the contest, Whale, who won?

Whale: Appears from below and rests head on edge of stage left, panting. You did Rabbit. You may be small, but you are my equal. *Sinks below edge of stage with a groan.*

Rabbit: Rushes to stage right. Elephant! Am I, Rabbit, the small but mighty, the equal of Elephant, the large and loud?

Elephant: appears from below and rests head on edge of stage right, panting Oh yes, Rabbit. You are my equal. You really, really are. Excuse me, I have to go take a nap now. *slides down out of sight*

Rabbit: goes to center stage Did you hear that, Turtle? They said I was their equal. You and I have won a great victory for small animals everywhere.

Turtle: Yes! And now, Rabbit, let's go whip up a celery milkshake.

Rabbit: And some carrot fries! Oh, boys and girls. Thanks for your help. How about a cheer for Turtle. Yea Turtle. Woo-woo-woo!

Animals: Yea Turtle. Woo-woo-woo!

Turtle: Thank you, and this play is over. The end, the end, the end.

Playing Notes

Puppeteers and Puppets

Whale can be any large water animal. A crocodile would be a good substitute. The cheering section is made up of any animal puppets you have. They are positioned between the green and blue backdrops. These backdrops can be left out if you do not use the cheering section.

Classroom or Workshop Productions

In addition to assigning one puppeteer to each character, you will need two children to manage the buckets of confetti. The animal cheering section can be as large as you wish. Use face paint and surround masks for a very nice effect if you don't have many animal puppets. The Whale and Elephant puppets must be able to hold things in their mouths. A wide stage is most effective with this play. If you have a cut-out frame stage, consider draping a curtain over the top using the top of the stage for a playing area.

Library Production

Two puppeteers can perform this play, but you will need two helpers to throw the confetti. One puppeteer is Whale and Turtle; the other is Rabbit and Elephant. The helpers assist with the rope as well as with the confetti. Eliminate the animal cheering section and instruct the audience to cheer.

Props and Scenery

The confetti, which is actually small bits of paper rolled into tight wads, is messy but essential. The audience is astonished and then delighted as this "water," "foam," "sand," and "grass" fly from the struggling animals onto heads and laps. They may forget to cheer, so Turtle will have to remind them. Adults in the audience may remind the children to cheer. The more confetti you throw, the better and more hilarious the effect. A puppet helper must be stationed at each side of the stage to throw the confetti. Test the wads of paper to make sure they have enough weight to clear the top of the stage and land in the audience.

The rope should be thick enough to appear weighty but light enough for the puppets to handle. Try a fabric store that sells drapery supplies. The actual tugging must be well rehearsed. There must be enough tension on the rope to create the illusion of a contest, but not enough to pull the rope out of the puppet's mouth. It is very important to agree on a signal at which the Elephant and Whale drop the rope. They should drop it at the same moment. Someone backstage can start a countdown that the Whale and Elephant puppeteers will recognize, then make eye contact, and join in. It will be hard to hear, so eye contact and exaggerated mouthing of the numbers will be necessary. This should also be well rehearsed.

Decorate the front of the stage with paper cutouts of beach and ocean scenes for the Whale and with grassland scenes for the Elephant. For the water, attach white, blue, and green waves to the top edge. Attach fish, turtles, and water bugs further down to suggest depth. Mark the Elephant's side with spiky grasses on the top edge and cutouts of grassland animals on the stage curtains. In the center, jungle trees and plants decorate the stage curtains with brightly colored birds, monkeys, etc., hidden in the branches. At the top edge of the stage in the center, attach a palm tree with a narrow, tall trunk and lots of green frond shapes on the top. Use a piece of card stock strengthened with a dowel for the trunk. Green tissue paper is effective for the fronds. The tree must suggest a visual barrier between the Whale and the Elephant, but not obscure the Rabbit and the Turtle. Place a green backdrop at the rear of the stage, and a blue backdrop behind that. The blue backdrop is two feet higher. The cheering section is positioned between the two backdrops.

Action

Turtle and Rabbit are very active and bouncy during the tug-of-war. Whale and Elephant swing their heads and are loud, but do not move a great deal. The animal's cheering section looks from side to side during the contest, but does not move much. The actual tugging on the rope is important and tricky. Rehearse this action many times so that the puppeteers will know how to best achieve the effect of tension and strength.

Program Building

Library Programs

Demonstrate the tug-of-war to the children with some volunteers from the audience as an introduction to the play. *Story:* "The Tortoise and the Hare." *Read Aloud:* "Who's in Rabbit's House?" *Short Craft:* Children decorate three-inch discs of card stock that read "Small Is Great!" Attach the discs to a ribbon and wear them around the neck.

Longer Programs and Classroom Study Units

Explore the history of games and learn some other old-fashioned games that children today might not know. Create murals of river, pond, rain forest, and grassland scenes. Find out which animals live in these habitats and how they adapt to their habitats. Read *Aesop's Fables.* There are many stories of small animals succeeding in contests with larger animals by using trickery. Many of the Brer Rabbit stories are of this type. Collect many examples for the classroom. Illustrate them and act them out. Show students that problems can be worked out in innovative ways that are not violent and do not rely on physical strength.

Bibliography

Picture Books

Amazing Bone. William Steig. Farrar, Straus and Giroux, 1971. (1–4)

Hot Hippo. Mwenye Hadithi. Little, Brown, 1986. (P–1)

Loudmouse. Richard Wilbur. Crowell Collier, 1968. (P–1)

Tortoise and the Hare: An Aesop Fable. Janet Stevens, adapter. Holiday House, 1984. (K–2)

Longer Fiction

Amos and Boris. William Steig. Farrar, Straus and Giroux, 1971. (2–4)

The Hostage. Theodore Taylor. Delacorte, 1988. (5–8)

How the Elephant Got Its Trunk. Rudyard Kipling. Harcourt Brace Jovanovich, 1983. (K–3)

How the Whale Got Its Throat. Rudyard Kipling. P. Bedrick Books, 1987. (K–2)

S.O.R. Losers. Avi. Bradbury, 1984. (5–7)

Nonfiction

Games

The Best Singing Games for Children of All Ages. Edgar S. Bley. Sterling, 1959. (1–5)

Games and How to Play Them. Anne Rockwell. Harper, 1973. (P–2)

The Games They Played: Sports in History. Richard Lyttle. Atheneum, 1982.

Juba This and Juba That. Revised Edition. Virginia Tashjian. Little, Brown, 1995. (K–4)

What Are Street Games. Anthony Ravialli. Atheneum, 1981.

Animals

Album of Whales: Animals. Tom Mcgowen. Macmillan, 1980. (4–6)

Discovering Rabbits and Hares. Keith Porter. Watts, 1986. (4–6)

Elephants. Norman Barrett. Watts, 1988. (3–6)

Elephants. Cynthia Overbeck. Lerner, 1987. (4–7)

Elephants. Elsa Posell. Childrens Press, 1982. (1–4)

Killer Whales and Dolphins Play. Don Torgensen. Childrens Press, 1982. (4–6)

Turtle Watch. George Ancona. Macmillan, 1987. (2–5)

Turtles and Tortoises. Vincent Serventy. Raintree, 1985. (1–4)

Whales. Gilda Berger. Doubleday, 1987. (2–4)

Whales of the World. June Behrens. Childrens Press, 1987. (1–3)

Whales, the Nomads of the Sea. Helen Sattler. Lothrop, 1987. (3–7)

Poems

Inside Turtle's Shell and Other Poems of the Field. Joanne Ryder. Macmillan, 1985. (1-4)

Stories

Knee High Man and Other Tales. Julius Lester. Dial, 1972. (K–2)

Tales of Uncle Remus: The Adventures of Brer Rabbit. Julius Lester. Dial, 1987. (4–8)

Zajota and the Boogie Spirit (video recording). Ayoka Chenzira. Modern Educational Video Network, 1992. (3–7)

2

Coyote and Hawk Put
The Sun and Moon in Place
and
Coyote Steals the Spring

Performers: grades 4 through 8
Audience: grades K through 4
Cast: Narrator
Coyote
Hawk
Bear
Snake
Frog
Rabbit
Woman

Props: Two balls of grass, one slightly larger; sun and moon (reverse side of balls of grass); bags for spring, summer, fall, and winter; hat for narrator in "Coyote Steals the Spring."
Set: Forest—patch of dried grass in center. Tipi—(open front) at far stage right in "Coyote Steals the Spring."

Narrator: According to Native American stories, when the earth began there were no people, just animals, and Coyote was the most important of the animals. Coyote had to do many things to prepare the land for the coming of the people. He put fish in the rivers, berries and roots in the earth, trees in the forests. It was Coyote, with help from Hawk, who put the sun and moon in the sky and gave light to the world. Then Coyote ended a long and terrible winter by stealing the spring. When our play begins it is very dark. You will be able to see, but remember, Hawk and Coyote cannot see each other at all.

Exit narrator stage right. There is very little light. Coyote enters stage left and Hawk enters stage right. There are sounds of animals colliding, grunts and bangs as they fall.

Hawk: Ouch! Who is that? *Animals touch each other.* Is that you, Coyote?

Coyote: Yes. Is that you Hawk?

Lights come up a bit.

Hawk: It's me. I'm sorry I bumped into you. It is so dark, I can't see a thing. You nearly scared the feathers off of me.

Coyote: It wasn't your fault, Hawk. I couldn't see either, or I would have kept my long nose out of your way.

Hawk: Wouldn't it be wonderful if there were light in the world, and we could see where we are going, and what we look like? What do you think you look like, Coyote?

Coyote: Well, I think I must be very handsome. I know I have a very fine tail. I wish there were light too. I think that the people will not like so much darkness when they come to the world. *Sigh.* Oh well, it doesn't do any good to be sad.

Hawk: I know that, but I can't help being sad. I think I'll just lie down in this tule grass and cry a little. *Sniff.*

Coyote: Oh, my poor friend. Wait a minute. Maybe we could use that tule grass to make a light in the world!

Hawk: This old marsh grass? How could we light the world with this?

Coyote: I'm not sure. Let's begin by forming it into a ball. Hold it steady on that side. *Patting and grunting.* Now. It's ready. You take it in your claws, Hawk, and I will set fire to the bottom of it.

Hawk: Set fire to it? While I am holding it in my claws? Unh, unh. No way. Never.

Coyote: Wait, listen. You fly with it up into the sky—as high as you can—and just before the fire touches your feet . . .

Hawk: Sooner than that maybe.

Coyote: I will watch very carefully, and before the fire touches you, I will shout "Let go, Hawk!" And you will leave the ball burning in the sky. Then you fly back to earth.

Hawk: Oh, all right. I'll try it. But remember my feet and claws are important to me.

Coyote: You are a brave creature, Hawk. Hold the ball. I will light the fire with this flint. Now, up, Hawk! Up, up, up! Let go!

Hawk rises up with the ball and releases it, then swoops to stage right and exits. The ball turns to the sun side and remains in the sky. All lights are turned on at this point.

Hawk: Returns panting; walking on from stage right. I held on as long as I could, but it got really hot. How does it look? Will it work?

Coyote: Look at it, friend!

Hawk: Ohh! That is a fine light. How warm and bright it is.

Coyote: And we can see the world. How beautiful the world is. And how handsome you are, Hawk. Your eyes are yellow, and your feathers black and white. We must name this light. Let's call this light "sun."

Hawk: Sun—I like that. The people will love the sun when they come. Oh no! Sun is sinking out of the sky.

Sun goes down.

Coyote: That is called "sunset." Isn't sunset beautiful.

Hawk: Yes, but now it seems colder and darker than ever.

Coyote: It would be a good idea to have a smaller light in the sky at night. That way the people could sleep but the night animals would be able to see to get food and water.

Hawk: Good idea. Are we going to do that thing with the grass and fire again?

Coyote: Yes, but the ball of grass will be much smaller and the fire not as hot. Let's make the grass ball. *They work.*

17

Hawk: There. It's done, I think. I will hold it and you light the fire. *Coyote lights the fire and Hawk flies up.*

Coyote: Up, Hawk, up, up, up. Now let go!

Hawk rises up with ball and lets go. It turns to moon side. Hawk swoops to the right and exits. Hawk then returns panting from stage right.

Hawk: How does this one look?

Coyote: Oh Hawk! You are some bird! Look at that!

Hawk: Oh my! This one is as beautiful as the sun.

Coyote: One is powerful and warm and golden, the other is gentle and cool and silver. The people will love them both.

Hawk: What shall we call this light?

Coyote: I don't know. Why don't we ask those girls and boys out there?

Hawk: Girls and boys? *Looks at the children.* Squawk!

Coyote: Boys and girls, what should we name this light?

All: Moon!

Hawk: Moon. That sounds perfect.

Moon and Sun change places in the sky as Coyote and Hawk watch.

Coyote: I just made up a song for the sun. It goes like this:
Ha ha sun.
Ha ha rain.
Ha Ha seeds.
Ha ha grain.

Moon and Sun change places again.

Hawk: I like that song. I made up a song for the moon too. It's short. It goes like this:
So long
Moon song.

Moon and Sun change places again. Sounds of crashing and grunting and growling. Enter Bear, Snake, and Frog from stage left.

Bear: Coyote! We want to talk to you about these lights you and Hawk put in the sky.

Coyote: Talk away, Bear. I'm going to watch them go up and down and make up more songs.

Bear: Well, yes. It's that going up and down that we want to talk about.

Frog: They are wonderful lights. But we don't know when to sleep, or when to get food . . .

Snake: Or when to give birth to our young ones, or when to migrate.

Bear: We are confused, and bears do not like to be confused.

Coyote: I'm sorry, my friends. You must tell me what you want. How long should the sun be in the sky? How long should the moon shine? Tell me.

Snake: Ten years. Ten years of sun and ten years of moon.

Bear: One year. A year of sun and a year of moon.

Frog: No, no, no, that is not right. When the people come they will not want long darkness and long days. They will want one short darkness and one short day. One darkness, one day. One darkness, one day.

Coyote: Frog is right. The people will like that best. One darkness and one day. Twelve hours each. Sun, stay in the sky for twelve hours. Moon, when sun leaves, you stay in the sky for twelve hours. *Sun stays in the sky and the moon stays down.*

Coyote: There. That will do for now. Later I will figure out how the moon will change shape and where the stars will go. Now I have to go do something about the seasons. *Coyote exits stage right.*

Bear: Thanks, Coyote. Hey, I saw some great berry bushes by that river over there. Let's go check them out.

All exit stage left. A sign is held up reading "Coyote Steals the Spring."

Coyote Steals the Spring

Narrator: Enters stage left. After Coyote sorted out night and day, things were very peaceful for a while. The people came to live in the world and were happy. They took good care of the land and the animals. It was said that there was a woman who kept the four seasons in leather pouches in her home. *Platform with this scene on it is raised to stage level on far stage left.* There they hung from the roof—a pouch for winter, a pouch for spring, a pouch for summer, and a pouch for fall. If it was time for fall to change into winter, she would take down the winter bag, open it, and let the winter—cold and snow and winds and ice—out upon the world. Fall would be driven back home and back to its bag. She decided when it was time for the seasons to change. When winter had gone on long enough, when spring should become summer and summer, fall. Often the people did not agree with her about how long the seasons were to be, especially the winter, but they did not dare to argue with the woman, who was very clever and powerful. When our play begins, it had been winter for a very long time. In fact, I feel a little cold right now. Excuse me for a moment. *Exits stage right and returns with winter hat on.* The people and animals were cold and hungry. They had used up all the food they had put away for winter. This is the story of what Coyote did to steal the spring and end the winter. *Exit Narrator.*

Woman stirs. She looks at each of the bags.

Woman: Heh, heh, heh. Spring, summer, and fall still in their bags. Winter is still out. It's nice and cold. *Lies down and snores.*

Enter Coyote stage right, shivering and bouncing up and down, repeating "Cold, cold, cold, cold." Enter Bear stage right hunting around the ground.

Bear: Hi, Coyote. Have you seen any acorns or seeds? My people have nothing left to eat. *groan* If only winter would end. If only spring would come.

Coyote: I don't have any food either. No nuts, no seeds, no berries, no grain. Winter just goes on and on and on.

Bear: Don't you have even a wrinkled old apple core you could share with a hungry bear?

Coyote: No I don't. We'll just have to go hungry until the old woman lets the spring out. There's nothing we can do. Nothing! *Sighs.*

Loud snore from old woman's tent. Coyote looks toward tent.

Coyote: We just have to go hungry until . . . *another snore.* Bear, come here. *They lean their heads together.* I have an idea about how to end the winter.

Bear: *Loud.* End winter? Really, how?

Coyote: Shhh! *Glances toward old woman's tent.* We'll steal the spring from the old woman's tent and let it out.

Bear: How? She's clever, and mean. If she catches us, we're done for.

Coyote: Well, we'll steal the spring while she's asleep. She won't know that it's gone until she wakes up.

Bear: That's a great idea, Coyote, but we'll need help. We need someone who is silent, quick, and brave. *Rabbit creeps in stage right.* Someone who doesn't make a noise. Someone who is not afraid.
Rabbit taps Bear on the back. Bear screams and runs behind Coyote.

Bear: Aiyeee!

Coyote: Hi, Rabbit. You sure scared this tiny little bear.

Bear: She just surprised me, that's all.

Rabbit: I hear you need someone silent, brave, and quick. How about me? I'm silent, brave, and quick.

Coyote: We're sick of the winter, and we want to steal the spring from the old woman over there and let it out.

Rabbit: Great idea! But how will we do it? Bear's right. That woman is mean and smart.

Coyote: Well, let me think. *Puts head to one side, then the other.* Okay, I've got it. Listen up. *They put heads together.* Rabbit, you're quick and silent. You sneak into the old woman's tent, grab the bag with the spring in it, and run out of the tent. You pass the bag to me, and hide. I can run for long distances, so I take the bag and run to Bear, then I hide. Bear is really strong, so he tears open the bag and lets the spring out.

Bear: Wait, Coyote, what happens if the old woman wakes up and says magic words or something?

Coyote: Hmmm, well . . .

Rabbit: I know. When I sneak into the tent, I have a comb of honey in one paw. I smack the old woman on the mouth with the honey. It sticks her lips together, and she can't say magic words. Then I grab the spring bag.

Coyote: Great idea! Okay. Let's practice. You stand there, Rabbit. *Points stage left.* And you stand over there Bear. *Points stage right.* I'll stay right here. Now, Rabbit, you pretend to steal the bag, pass it to me, and I'll pass it to Bear. Okay, go!

Rabbit: Okay. Sneak, honey, bag, run, pass. *Mimes action and hits Coyote's nose.*

Coyote: Oww! Rabbit, take it easy. Be careful.

Rabbit: Sorry, sorry. Let's try it again.

Coyote: Okay, everybody ready? Bear?

Bear: Bear has fallen asleep and is snoring.

Coyote: Bear!

Bear: What? Oh, ready.

Coyote: Great. Keep alert. Okay, Rabbit, go for it.

Rabbit: Here we go. Sneak into tent, smack with honey, grab bag, run, and pass. *Mimes action from left to right.*

Coyote: Take bag, run, pass to Bear. *Mimes also.*

Bear: Take bag, tear it open, let out spring.

Coyote: Fantastic! We're ready! Everybody be very, very quiet.

The three approach the old woman's tent. Coyote pushes Bear back to far stage right. Coyote moves to center stage. Bear and Coyote sink down until only the tops of their heads show. Rabbit moves stage left and waits at entrance to tent, then sneaks into tent.

Old Woman: Snores and then says Humph! What was that? Hey!

Rabbit smacks old woman with honey.

Old Woman: Hmmm. Yum!

Rabbit grabs bag and runs toward center stage.

Rabbit: Coyote, where are you?

Coyote: Right here, Rabbit. Pass the bag, Rabbit. There! *Rabbit hides center stage.*

Coyote: Here I come, Bear.

Bear: I'm ready. *Grabs bag in mouth as Coyote hides.* Grr, grr, grr. *Drops bag behind stage.* The spring is out. The spring is out!

Birds chirp and flowers pop up. Coyote and Rabbit come back onstage.

Coyote: Hey, it's warmer already.

Rabbit: I can hear the grass growing.

Bear: It's spring! We did it Coyote. We did it.

Coyote: Yep, we did it, And now our play is over.

All three: The end. The end. The end.

Playing Notes

Puppeteers and Puppets

Classroom Production

Many children can be involved. Each puppeteer handles only one puppet. The Hawk puppeteer must wear a black sleeve to strengthen the illusion that Hawk flies. Other children handle the props, produce sound effects, and manage lights. Slide whistles accompany the rising and sinking of the sun and moon. Increase the number of the puppets who complain about the sun and moon. More animal puppets can welcome the spring. Attach birds and butterflies to rods with string or to flexible metal rods. They flit over the stage when spring appears. Toss flowers over the top of the stage and into the audience.

Library Production

This play can be performed by two puppeteers and a helper. Give the part of the narrator to one of the lesser characters, like Bear. The animals that complain about the sun and moon are reduced to two, Bear and Frog. One puppeteer is Hawk, Bear, and the voice of the woman. The other is Coyote, Frog, and Rabbit. The helper moves the sun and moon up and down. The helper can also move the woman in the tent. She is attached to the tent set with a rod extending from the bottom of the set so that she appears to move slightly in sleep and to struggle a bit with Rabbit.

Props and Scenery

Decorate the stage front with trees, bushes, rocks, marsh grass, and streams to create a woodland scene. Far stage left must be kept clear for the tent set, which will be added for the second story. At center stage, marsh grass grows right up to stage edge. For the sun and moon, cut four circles of cardboard, one pair eight inches in diameter and the other pair four inches. Glue the matching circles together with a rod glued between the two circles and sticking out about two feet. Paint the larger one yellow and orange on one side. On the other side, glue some dry grass, or paper shredded to resemble

dry grass. Paint the smaller circle silver on one side and glue the same grassy material to the other side. At the bottom of the discs, where the rod sticks out, attach a few orange and yellow streamers to the sun. Attach silver and blue streamers to the moon. They will not be seen until Hawk flies up. At that point they create the illusion of flames.

In the second story, Rabbit simply pretends to have honey in his paw. The pouch with spring in it is an important prop. Make it large and light so that the puppets can handle it easily. Brown or tan felt makes a good pouch. Paint the word "Spring" on the bag. Paint "Fall" and "Summer" on the other bags. The fall and summer bags are not moved and should be attached to the set, out of the way of the action. You need not make a winter bag since it is winter in the world.

The tent set is a cutaway section of a tipi made of a stiff fabric like felt or burlap. It is glued to a piece of cardboard that serves as a floor. It must be very open at the front so that Rabbit can reach in and put honey on the woman's mouth and grab the spring bag. How you attach this set to the stage will depend upon the design of your stage. It can be as simple as a painted backdrop with the woman and spring bag attached. The tent set should be just big enough to hold the woman and the pouches, and put up as far to stage left as can be managed without creating sight line problems. This leaves maximum room for the action of the other puppets.

With two puppeteers the helper must create the spring alone. Mount clumps of flowers cut from colored paper on a three-foot measure or a section of lathe and hold this up to the stage level when Bear lets the spring out. Blow bird whistles at the same time. Distribute bird whistles and paper flowers to the audience and instruct them to blow the whistles and throw the flowers when spring comes.

Action

Practice the movement of Hawk flying up with the sun and moon many times. It is important to the feeling of the play that Hawk's flight, the movement of the sun and moon, and Coyote's words blend together perfectly. Hawk only appears to grip the ball of grass. Simply hold the bottom of the puppet against the disc. As Hawk "releases" the sun and moon, turn the grass side slowly to reveal the sun and moon side. The sun and moon continue to rise a little more. The puppeteer may have to stand on a stool to get some height for Hawk's flight.

The rising and sinking of the sun and moon are not random. They must match the words of the puppets. The rising and sinking should be slow—to the count of one and two and three and four. At the end of the story, the sun remains in the sky. If you have a helper to do it, the sun can be raised again when the spring appears in the second story. The action in the spring story is simple but important, and must be well rehearsed. The woman in the tent should snore loudly and move slightly. She could chuckle menacingly when the animals talk about her. The characters' practice session is somewhat silly and slapsticky. Take some time with Rabbit sneaking up to and into the tent. Coyote might bobble the pouch a bit when it is passed to him. Bear should growl a lot and flail about as he tears open the spring bag. All the puppets dance and cheer when the spring appears.

Program Building

Library Programs

You may want to have an interlude between the two stories and tell a tale about the stars. *Stories:* Learn and tell a Native American story or a story from another culture about the sun, moon, or seasons, such as "We Want Sunshine in Our Houses" or "Little Sister and the Month Brothers." *Read Aloud:* "Arrow to the Sun" by Gerald McDermott or "Iktomi and the Boulder" by Paul Goble. Invite participation in this by having the audience imitate the sound of the bats. *Short Craft:* Make a musical instrument (rattle or drum) that Native Americans might use. Make stick puppets of the sun and moon. *Music:* Play a tape of Native American music. Teach and sing a simple song about the sun, moon, or seasons. "The Eency Weency Spider" is good for very young audiences.

Classroom Study Units

There are many excellent collections of Native American stories appropriate for children. Many of the stories deal with issues that concern today's students and their families. They teach respect for family, community, and the environment. Many are short and could be learned and told by older children. Create workstations in the classroom that focus on the many areas of study suggested by the stories in this play and in story collections. Some suggestions for workstations might be the environment, astronomy, American history, Native American folk stories, and the effect of light and the seasons on people and animals. Folk stories from other cultures about the sun, moon, stars, and seasons, and a display of the constellations with their Native American names, would also be effective workstations. Find and/or write poems and songs about the sun, moon, and stars.

Bibliography

Picture Books

And Me Coyote. Betty Baker. Macmillan, 1982. (K–3)

Before You Came This Way. Byrd Baylor. Dutton, 1969. (2–4)

Borreguita and the Coyote. Verna Aardema. Knopf, 1991. (K-2)

Coyote Goes Hunting for Fire. Margery Bernstein and Janet Kobrin. Scribner's, 1974. (K-2)

Doctor Coyote. John Bierhorst. Macmillan, 1987. (K–2)

Hawk, I'm Your Brother. Byrd Baylor. Scribner's, 1976. (3–5)

How the Sun Made a Promise and Kept It. Margery Bernstein and Janet Kobrin. Scribner's, 1974. (K–2)

Iktomi and the Boulder—A Plains Indian Story. Paul Goble. Orchard/Watts, 1988. (Use any Paul Goble title.) (2–5)

Little Sister and the Month Brothers. Beatrice Schenk De Regniers. Seabury, 1976. (K–2)

Moon Song. Byrd Baylor. Scribner's, 1982 (K–3)

The Way to Start a Day. Byrd Baylor. Scribner's, 1978. (K–4)

Why the Sun and Moon Live in the Sky. Elphinstone Dayrell. Houghton Mifflin, 1968. (K–3)

Longer Fiction

Anpao. Jamake Highwater. Lippincott, 1977. (5–8)

Beyond the Ridge. Paul Goble. Bradbury, 1989. (3–5)

Island of the Blue Dolphins. Scott O'Dell. Houghton Mifflin, 1960. (5–8)

Moonsong Lullaby. Jamake Highwater. Lothrop, 1981. (5–8)

Morning Girl. Michael Dorris. Hyperion, 1992. (4–6)

The Raid. G. Clifton Wisler. Dutton, 1985. (5–8)

Streams to the River, River to the Sea. Scott O'Dell. Houghton Mifflin, 1986. (5–8)

Sweetgrass. Jan Hudson. Putnam, 1989. (5–8)

Waterless Mountain. Laura Armer. McKay, 1931. (5–7). (Newbery Medal)

Nonfiction

Native American Studies

American Indian Music and Musical Instruments. George S. Fichter. McKay, 1978. (4–8)

American Indians Sing. Charles Hoffmann. Harper and Row, 1967. (3–6)

Animals in Winter. Susanna Riha. Carolrhoda, 1989. (3–4)

Animals in Winter. Ronald M. Fisher. National Geographic Society, 1982. (3–6)

Astronomy. Dennis B. Fradin. Childrens Press, 1983. (1–4)

Bears. Norman Barrett. Watts, 1988. (3–6)

Black Bear: The Spirit of the Wilderness. Barbara Ford. Houghton Mifflin, 1981. (6–8)

Buffalo Hunt. Russell Freedman. Holiday, 1988. (4–8)

The Controversial Coyote. Laurence Pringle. Harcourt Brace and Co., 1977. (6–8)

Do Not Disturb: Mysteries of Animal Hibernation and Sleep. Margery Facklam. Little, Brown, 1989. (3–5)

Eagles, Hawks, and Other Birds of Prey. Lynda Dewitt. Watts, 1989. (3–6)

Exploring the Sky: 100 Projects for Beginning Astronomers. Richard Moeschl. Chicago Review, 1989. (5–8)

First Came the Indians. M. J. Wheeler. Macmillan, 1983. (2–4)

The First Travel Guide to the Moon: What to Pack, How to Go, and What to See When You Get There. Rhonda Blumberg. Macmillan, 1980. (5–8)

From Abenaki to Zuni: A Dictionary of Native American Tribes. Evelyn Olofson. Walker, 1988. (4–8)

Happily May I Walk: American Indians and

Alaska Natives Today. Arlene Hirschfelder. Macmillan, 1986. (5–8)

How the Plains Indians Lived. George S. Fichter. McKay, 1980. (5–8)

Indians. Edwin Tunis. Harper and Row, 1979. (4–8)

To Live in Two Worlds: American Indian Youth Today. Brent Ashabranner. Dodd Mead, 1984. (5–8)

The Long View into Space. Seymour Simon. Crown, 1979. (3–5)

Macmillan Book of Astronomy. Roy A. Gallant. Macmillan, 1986. (3–7)

Native American Cookbook. Edna Henry. Messner, 1983. (3–7)

The Reasons for Seasons. Linda Allison. Little, Brown, 1975. (1–5)

Science of the Early American Indians. Beulah and Harold Tannenbaum. Watts, 1988. (5–8)

Sun Days and Shooting Stars: A Skywatcher's Calendar. Franklyn M. Branley. Houghton Mifflin, 1980. (4–6)

The Sun: Our Nearest Star. Franklyn M. Branley. Harper and Row, 1988. (1–3)

Sun Up, Sun Down. Gail Gibbons. Harcourt Brace, 1983. (1–3)

The Tipi: A Center of Native American Life. Charlotte Yue. Knopf, 1984. (4–7)

Biographies

Indian Chiefs. Russell Freedman. Holiday House, 1987. (5–8)

Ishi, Last of His Tribe. Theodora Kroeber. Bantam, 1973. (5–7)

Ishi: The Last of His People. David Petersen. Children's Press, 1991. (–6)

People of the Short Blue Corn. Harold Courlander. Henry Holt, 1996. (4–8)

Story Collections

Why the Possum's Tail Is Bare: And Other North American Indian Nature Tales. James E. Connolly. Stemmer, 1985. (4–7)

They Dance in the Sky: Native American Star Myths. Jean Guard Monroe. Houghton Mifflin, 1987. (4–8)

Music

Earth Spirit: Native American Flute. R. Carlos Nakai. Canyon Records, 1987. (compact disc)

3

The Elves and the Shoemakers

Performers: grades 5 through 8
Audience: grades K–4

Cast: Narrator
       Husband
       Wife
       Elf I: Ellie
       Elf II: Eddie
       Little Red Riding Hood (LRRH)
       Rabbit (costumed as Santa Claus)
       King Balthazar

Props: Shoes, leather, bag of groceries, elf suits, cloth for elf suits.

Set: A cobblers' shop with a Christmas tree on far stage right.

Narrator: Many years ago, people didn't go to stores to buy shoes, you know. All shoes were made by hand, and the people who made shoes were called shoemakers, or cobblers. Shoemakers would buy big pieces of leather, cut them into shapes, and sew the shapes into shoes. Then they would sell the shoes. There was once a husband and wife who were shoemakers. Through bad luck, they found themselves very poor. All they had left in their shop was one small piece of leather, enough to make one pair of shoes. That's where our puppet play begins, in the poor shoemakers' shop on December 21. Remember that date—December 21. *Exit stage left.*

Enter husband and wife stage right.

Husband: Ah, things are not good, dear. This is all the leather we have. We can make only one more pair of shoes. I hope they are bought quickly so we can buy another bit of leather.

Wife: Don't be discouraged. Let's cut them out tonight and stitch them up tomorrow. We'll sing while we work to cheer us up.

They work, singing "We Three Kings."
Husband: We three kings of Orient are . . .

Wife: Bearing gifts we travel so far. La la, la, . . .

Husband: There, that's finished. *yawning*

Wife: Let's sleep now and let tomorrow bring us a new day and better luck.

Exit Husband and Wife stage right. Enter elves popping up from below at center stage.

Ellie: I think that these shoemakers need our help. What can we do?

Eddie: Well, we could sew up these shoes while they sleep. That might make things a bit easier for them.

Sounds of tapping and hammering—elves make sewing and hammering motions.

Ellie: Sew and sew, tap and tap.

Eddie: Stitch and stitch, and that is that—finished. *Puts pair of shoes on counter.*

Ellie: Very nice. Very, very nice. Even if I do say so myself.

Eddie: Time to go. Bye.

Ellie: Good luck, shoemakers!

Elves exit with a hop up and quick sinking down at stage center. Sign appears stage left and moves across to exit stage right. It reads "December 22." Enter shoemakers stage right.

Wife: What a fine day. Let's begin to work on the shoes.

Husband: I think it will be a lucky day. Oh look, the leather we cut out last night has been stitched up and finished!

Wife: What tiny stitches. Why, this is very fine work.

Husband: Joking tone to wife. Did you finish these shoes while I slept?

Wife: Of course not, you silly. You worked on them in the night, and now you're playing a trick on me.

Husband: No I didn't. *They hug.* Never mind. Here comes a customer who might buy these fine shoes.

Wife: Oh dear, it's that chatterbox, Little Red Riding Hood. I'll go get breakfast started.

Exit Wife stage right. Bell sounds. Enter Little Red Riding Hood from far stage left.

LRRH: Hello, I'm Little Red Riding Hood. I'm looking for some shoes for my grandmother. I think that those will do nicely. *Gestures to shoes on counter.* She hates those sensible granny shoes, you know. She likes shoes with a bit of zip to them. My, my, what beautiful work. These will be perfect for Granny. You know, shoemaker, I have been wanting some red shoes to match my beautiful cape. Don't you think it's lovely? Don't I look stunning in it? Anyway, do you think you could make me a pair of red shoes to go with my red cape?

Husband: Why certainly. They'll be ready tomorrow afternoon.

LRRH: Very good. Here's your money. Deliver the shoes to Granny. You can't miss her house. I will tell Cinderella and everyone about your fine work. *Exit far stage left.*

Wife: Enters. Has she gone? Did she buy the shoes?

Husband: Yes. She paid cash, and she ordered another pair. *Removes shoes from counter.* Let's go out and buy more leather, some red for Little Red Riding Hood, and maybe a bit of shiny black to go with the brass buckles I have been saving. And you know, I think that there will be enough money left over to buy some food for a Christmas feast.

Wife: Wonderful. We will buy figs, and nuts, and tangerines, and maybe a bit of honey.

Exit Husband and Wife far stage left. Sound of bell followed by a short pause. Husband and Wife enter far stage left with leather and food. Bell sounds again.

Husband: Our luck is changing, I can feel it. Why, we got these pieces of leather at such a good price there was plenty left over for food.

Wife: We will have a fine holiday feast. Only two more days until Christmas. Let's cut out the shoes tonight, and sew them in the morning.

Husband: Good idea. Just let me put these groceries away first. *Tosses bag of groceries behind him.* But I don't want you getting up in the night to sew them by candlelight, you silly goose.

Wife: Not me. *Husband and Wife sing "We Wish You a Merry Christmas" while working on shoes.*

Husband: That's done. The leather is all ready to stitch. *Puts pieces of leather on counter.*

Wife: Enough for three pairs of shoes. Tomorrow will be a busy day.

Husband and Wife exit stage right. Enter elves center stage as before.

Ellie: Look, more shoe leather—all cut out.

Eddie: This red leather must be for Little Red Riding Hood.

Ellie: Let's stitch them up! *Sound of tapping and hammering as elves recite*

Eddie: Sew and sew, tap and tap.

Ellie: Stitch and stitch, and that is that.

Eddie: All ready for Little Red Riding Hood. *Puts shoes on counter.*

Ellie: Next pair!

Eddie: Sew and sew, tap and tap.

Ellie: Stitch and stitch, and that is that.

Eddie: Oh! These are gorgeous gold shoes!

Ellie: Fine enough for a king. *Puts shoes on counter.*

Eddie: Okay. Now for pair number three.

Ellie: Sew and sew, tap and tap.

Eddie: Stitch and stitch, and that is that.

Ellie: Hmm. Shiny black boots. Who will want shiny black boots, do you suppose? *Puts shoes on counter.*

Eddie: Can't imagine. Oh, oh! It's time to go!

Exit elves center stage as before. Sign appears stage left and moves across to exit stage right. It reads "December 23."

Enter Husband and Wife stage right.

Husband: Let's begin stitching up that leather right away. We'll begin with the red ones so that they will be finished when Little Red Riding Hood comes in.

Wife: Oh my! Look at this! All the shoes are finished. Who could have done this? And what beautiful work.

Husband: Not I. I could not stitch so fast.

Wife: And such tiny stitches. We must find out who is stitching up our shoes.

Enter LRRH far stage left. Bell sounds.

Husband: Here is Little Red Riding Hood for her shoes.

LRRH: Good morning, good morning. I know, I know, I'm early, but I couldn't wait to see my red shoes. Are my red shoes ready? Are they beautiful? Will they be the perfect accessory to my red cape and show off my dainty little feet? Hmmm?

Wife: Here they are, my dear. *Gestures to shoes.*

LRRH: Ooo, mmmm. They are exquisite. And don't they look nice with my cape. Everyone will admire me. Everyone will ask "Who is that beautiful little girl in the red cape and red shoes?" Grandmother loved her shoes too, and now Mama wants a pair just like them, but green. Mama likes green. I like red. Here is your money. Bye. *Exits stage left, taking shoes.*

Husband: How she chatters and chatters.

Wife: And how she pays! And she placed another order for more shoes. Oh dear, look down the street. It's Balthazar, one of the three kings of Orient.

Husband: Why, so it is. Heavens, could it be? He's stopping at our shop, and he's coming in!

Enter Balthazar far stage left. Bell sounds.

Husband: Good morning, sir. *Bowing slightly.*

Balthazar: Good morning. *Bowing also.* Those gold shoes. They look very, well, ah, kingly. Do they happen to be a size 12B?

Husband: Why yes, they are. And they would look very fine on you.

Balthazar: Yes, yes, I believe they would. By the way, I am planning a journey with two other kings. We all need traveling boots. Could you make three pairs of traveling boots by next week, all size 12B? *Aside to audience.* All kings wear size 12B, you know.

Wife: Yes, certainly. We would be honored.

Balthazar: I will send a servant to collect my boots and pay for them. *Aside to audience.* Kings never carry money. They always wear size 12B, and they never carry money. These are kingly facts. *To shoemakers.* Good day, then, until next week. *Exits stage left.*

Wife: Heavens! Our luck has truly changed. Who will come for these, do you suppose?

Bell rings as Rabbit enters far stage left dressed as Santa Claus.

Rabbit: Ho, ho, ho.

Husband: Ho, ho, ho, Rabbit. You look wonderful. Why are you dressed as Santa Claus?

Rabbit: I really do look fine, don't I? Do you like my beard? I made it myself. I'm playing Santa Claus in the school play and I need some shiny black boots. Do you have any shiny black boots? *Pause.* Oh, look at these!

Wife: They would be perfect for you, Rabbit. And I think that they are just your size.

Rabbit: Picks up boots. They are perfect. Shiny black leather, brass buckles. Yes! I'm going to be the best Santa ever! *Rabbit exits far stage left singing "Jingle Bells"*

Husband: Ha, ha. Well, dear, tonight we must find out who finished the shoes.

Wife: Yes indeed, and I know how to do it. We'll leave a bit of leather out, and hide behind the Christmas tree and wait. We'll find out who the secret shoemakers are if it takes all night.

Husband: Good idea. Here's the leather. *Reaches behind him.* Now let's hide. *They hide behind the Christmas tree.*

Enter elves center stage as before.

Eddie: They have gone to bed—time for us to work.

Ellie: Oh, only enough leather for one pair of shoes tonight. Well, let's begin.

Eddie: Sew and sew, tap and tap.

Ellie: Stitch and stitch, and that is that.

Eddie: All finished. Off we go!

Elves exit center stage as before. Husband and Wife come out of hiding.

Husband: Elves! My stars and garters! Elves made the shoes.

Wife: And did you see? Those elves had no clothes on. Poor little shivery things, all naked like that.

Husband: Well, we can fix that. Let's make them clothes to thank them for their work.

Wife: Right! First thing in the morning, we'll go and buy cloth and sew up a suit for each of them.

Husband: And I will make each of them some tiny elf boots.

Husband and Wife exit stage right. Sign appears and moves as before. It reads "December 24." Enter Husband and Wife stage left with cloth.

Husband: This won't take long with both of us working. What a fine way to spend Christmas Eve.

Wife: Tomorrow morning, on Christmas Day, they will find these clothes waiting for them instead of pieces of leather to sew into shoes. They will be the finest-looking elves in the world! *They work.*

Husband: Almost done!

Wife: There, finished. Put them on the counter. Now we will hide behind the tree again and wait for the elves to come.

Husband and Wife put suits on counter and hide behind Christmas tree. Elves enter center stage as before.

Eddie: I hope that the shoemakers left more leather for us to stitch.

Ellie: What? No leather, but look at this!

Eddie: Suits! Beautiful suits. And they are just our size!

Ellie: They must be for us. How splendid we will look!

Husband and Wife come out and hug elves. Merry Christmas helping elves, merry Christmas!

Ellie: Thank you. Thank you for our beautiful suits and shoes.

Eddie: We'll never be cold again.

Husband: It is we who must thank you for sewing our shoes and changing our luck.

Wife: Now you put on those suits and get all warm and cozy while I fix us hot chocolate to drink. *Wife and elves exit stage right*

Husband: Merry Christmas, merry Christmas.

Exit Husband stage right. Enter Rabbit center stage with sign that reads "December 25."

Rabbit: Oh, would you like to know how the story ends? The elves put on their suits and they were the finest-looking elves in the world. The shoemakers' good luck continued, and they lived happily ever after. Little Red Riding Hood looked great in her shoes, and I was the best Santa ever. Everybody had a very merry Christmas and you must have a very merry Christmas too. The end, the end.

Playing Notes

Puppeteers and Puppets

Classroom Production

Each character has one puppeteer. Additional children handle props, move signs, and produce sound effects. To involve more children, add an attendant to accompany Balthazar, and a dog to accompany Little Red Riding Hood. A group of puppet carolers could sing Christmas carols both before and after the play.

Library Production

This play can be performed by two puppeteers and a helper if there is only one elf. One puppeteer plays both the Husband and Wife. The second puppeteer plays the elf and the customers. The elf lines are combined. (See appendix for this version.) The helper assists the second puppeteer with puppet changes, handles the props, and produces sound effects.

Props and Scenery

There are several props in this play and handling them can be tricky. The boots and shoes are made out of felt. Cut out two silhouette boot shapes, stitch them together, and stuff with a little cotton or tissue. Make red, yellow, black, purple, and green pairs. Stitch each pair together at the top edges with a long loose stitch so that the boots cannot separate. The pieces of "leather" are pieces of felt of the same colors. Glue or pin the second group together. It will make this group of several colors easier to handle.

The elf suits are simply an outline of a suit cut out of red felt. Details such as belts, buttons, and pockets are added with fabric paint or glued-on bits of felt. Use green, gold, and black felt.

The signs help suggest the passing of time. They are painted on stiff paper or card stock, or made of felt, wood, tin, or whatever you have. Practice the handling of props many times until it goes smoothly and the puppeteers are confident.

The set will be determined somewhat by the design of your puppet stage. A counter is useful to display the shoes as the elves make them. Put a piece of felt under the shoes to keep them from slipping. If your stage does not have a platform or flat edge on which to place props, you can create a shelf with a piece of stiff card, four inches by six inches, that extends out toward the audience from stage center. Fold a one-inch lip down to attach it to the stage front and another one-inch lip up in front to create an edge so the shoes cannot slip off. Support it by suspending it with fish line from the top of the stage, or from below with brackets made of stiff card. The front lip can be painted with a sign, e.g., "Shoes—Finest Quality." If you do not wish to do this, have the elves show the shoes to the audience, and then place them behind the stage as though in a cupboard. Change the dialogue to explain this. The shoemakers can then bring out each pair of shoes as they are asked for.

One side of the stage must have a Christmas tree big enough for the shoemakers to hide behind. The other side is the entrance to the shop through which the customers enter. There is no door; the shop bell announces the customer's entrance.

Action

The elves can be played by one person who alternates movement to indicate which elf is speaking. Using their names in the script is simply a device to help puppeteers remember which elf is speaking. Elf movement is very quick, but they must deliver their lines clearly and carefully. It helps to stop the movement while the elves are speaking. Little Red Riding Hood also must appear to move and speak quickly, but must be understood. King Balthazar is slow and ponderous. His movements are so limited that this puppet can be placed on a rod if you want to eliminate a puppet change.

Program Building

Library Programs

Music

"Twelve Days of Christmas." Ask twelve volunteers to stand at the front of the room holding large cards numbered one through twelve. Each child holds their number up as it is sung. Even the smallest children knows "Jingle Bells." *Read Aloud:* "Anansi and the Strange Moss Covered Rock." This hilarious African story can be read or told to celebrate Kwanzaa. *Stories:* "The First Schlemiel" is a very funny Jewish story. Tell it or some other Jewish story to celebrate Hanukah. *Short Craft:* Light and candles are common to most of the December celebrations. Explain the various candleholders and colors of candles specific to Hanukah and Kwanzaa. Have the children assemble a simple (and inexpensive) candleholder. Paint votive holders with glue and decorate with glitter. Give each child a candle to put in their holders. Turn this into a less expensive collage creation by using paper cut-out candles and holders. Adjust to suit your budget and the crowd you anticipate.

Classroom Study Units

The production of this play and the creation of a performance make a wonderful holiday classroom project. Include other December celebrations, such as Hanukah, Kwanzaa, Winter Solstice, and customs from other lands, to make it a multicultural program. In the weeks before the performance, children can make stick puppets, paper bag puppets, and hand puppets with which to sing holiday songs before and after the play. Puppets in national costume can introduce songs and poems for a group of puppet carolers to perform. For instance, a puppet in a paper Santa Lucia wreath could discuss Winter Solstice and introduce the song "Santa Lucia." These puppets need not be people puppets. Animal puppets dressed in costumes add a light and playful touch.

On paper bags that have been crumpled and flattened out, children can trace their feet and make shoes by gluing or stapling the pieces of a pattern together. Antique pattern books or costume patterns sometimes include shoe patterns. Elf hats and pointed elf ears could also be made. Dreidel games, Kwanzaa candleholders, sun kites, lanterns, and paper balloons would also be appropriate. Make paper Santa Lucia wreaths with paper candles. Of course, the preparation of simple holiday foods is always fun.

Bibliography

Picture Books

Africa Dream. Eloise Greenfield. Harper and Row, 1989. (K–3)

Anansi and the Strange Moss Covered Rock. Eric Kimmel. Holiday House, 1988. (K–2) *Arthur's Christmas.* Marc Brown. Little, Brown, 1984. (K–2)

Beni's First Chanukah. Jane Breskin Zalben. Henry Holt, 1988. (P–K)

Donkey's Dream. Barbara Helen Berger. Putnam, 1985. (K–3)

It Could Always Be Worse. Margot Zemach. Farrar, Straus and Giroux, 1990. (1–4)

Just Enough Is Plenty. Barbara Goldin. Viking, 1988. (1–3)

Laughing Latkes. M. B. Goffstein. Farrar, Straus and Giroux, 1980. (K–3)

Pigs at Christmas. Arlene Dubanevich. Bradbury, 1986. (P–3)

Potato Pancakes All Around: A Hanukkah Tale. Marilyn Hirsh. Jewish Publication Society, 1978. (P–3)

Longer Fiction

Bells of Christmas. Virginia Hamilton. Harcourt Brace Jovanovich, 1989. (3–6)

Have a Happy . . . Mildred P. Walter. Lothrop, 1989. (3–6)

Justin and the Best Biscuits in the World. Mildred P. Walter. Lothrop, 1986. (2–5)

Night Journey. Kathryn Lasky. Viking, 1986. (4–7)

The Return. Sonia Levitin. Fawcett, 1988. (6–10)

Nonfiction

Christmas Gift. Charlemae Rollins. Follett, 1963. (4–8)

Hanukkah. June Behrens. Children's Press, 1983. (K–3)

Kwanzaa. Deborah Chocolate. Children's Press, 1990. (K–5)

Kwanzaa: Everything You Always Wanted to Know. Cedric McClester. Gumbs and Thomas, 1990. (5–8)

Light Another Candle: The Story and Meaning of Hanukkah. Miriam Chaikin. Houghton Mifflin, 1981. (3–8)

A Picture Book of Hanukkah. David Adler. Holiday, 1982. (P–3)

The Road to Bethlehem: An Ethiopian Nativity. Elizabeth Laird. Henry Holt, 1987. (1–5)

Cookbooks

The Children's Jewish Holiday Kitchen. Joan Nathan. Schocken, 1987. (4–8)

Cooking the African Way. Constance Nabuire. Lerner, 1988. (5–8)

Holiday Cooking Around the World. Lerner, 1988. (3–8)

Stories

Legend of Old Befana. Tomie de Paola, reteller. Harcourt, 1980. (P–3)

Lion and the Ostrich Chicks and Other African Folk Tales. Ashley Bryan. Macmillan, 1986. (3–5)

Naftali the Storyteller and His Horse, Sus and Other Stories. Isaac B. Singer. Farrar, Straus and Giroux, 1976. (3–12) (Any collection by Singer)

Tales of Uncle Remus. Julius Lester. Dial, 1987. (4–8) (Any collection by Lester)

4

Little Red Riding Hood

Performers: grades 3 through 4
Audience: preschool through grade 3

Cast: Narrator
Mother
Grandmother
Woodsman
Little Red Riding Hood (LRRH)
Wolf
Animal Chorus

Props: Basket for Little Red Riding Hood, nightcap for Wolf, wooden mallet for Woodsman

Set: A forest center stage, LRRH's house stage left, Grandmother's house stage right.

Narrator steps forward from the Chorus, center stage.

Narrator: Once upon a time, a little girl lived with her mother on the edge of a forest. Her grandmother lived in a cottage on the other edge of the forest. *Indicates houses.* In the forest there lived a big, bad . . . wolf!

Chorus: A wolf! There's a wolf! Ooooh!

Narrator: That's right, a big bad wolf. Now this little girl was very, very vain. That means she thought about how pretty she was all the time. She looked in mirrors, and store windows, and ponds, and patted her hair, and straightened her dress, and generally was just plain silly about her looks. Once she saw a woman who was wearing a red cape with a hood, and she fussed and begged until her mother made her a red cape with a hood. After that she was called Little Red Riding Hood, and no one even remembers her real name. Well, one day, her mother called her in from playing. This is what happened that day.

Narrator moves back into Chorus. Enter Little Red Riding Hood followed by Mother, stage left.

Mother: Little Red Riding Hood, I've just had word that your Granny is very sick and cannot get out of her bed. I want you to go through the forest to her cottage and take this basket of fruit and cakes and eggs and honey to her.

LRRH: All right, Mommy. I'll wear my red cape and hood, and my green boots, and . . .

Mother: It doesn't matter what you wear, dear. *Sigh.* Just get there quickly and safely. You are to follow the path straight to Granny's, and straight back. You are not to speak to anybody. And you are not to stray from the path.

LRRH: I won't. Granny will hardly know me in my new red riding hood. Why, the sight of me will probably make her completely well!

Mother: Oh dear! Well, when you get back we will have a talk about your cape, darling. Remember! No talking and no straying! Just there and back.

LRRH: O.K. Bye, Mommy.

LRRH starts to move to center stage while singing "Over the River and Through the Woods." Mother exits stage left.

Animal Chorus: Watch LRRH and make approving noises. She is pretty, isn't she? Lovely! And sweet. I hope she heeds her mother's advice.

LRRH: Ohh, look at that butterfly. And that one. And that one too. How beautiful. And look at those flowers. I'm sure Granny would like some of them.

Wolf appears from below stage level, just behind LRRH.

Animal Chorus: Hiss. Boo! Villain!

Wolf ignores them. He watches LRRH as she looks at flowers. He taps her on the shoulder.

LRRH: Turns to face Wolf. Oh, help!

Wolf: Do not be alarmed, my dear. What are you doing all alone in the forest? Don't you know that these woods are full of wild beasts? What are you carrying in that basket? I'm sure it must be much too heavy for a delicate child like you. And wherever did you get that stunning red cape? You look quite charming in it.

LRRH: Why, thank you, Mr. Wolf. I'm on my way to my Granny's. She is not well, and I must take her this basket of food. It really isn't very heavy at all.

Wolf: What a brave little girl you are. But if your Granny is sick in bed, who will let you into the cottage?

LRRH: I tap on the door four times and say "Granny it's me," and she will tell me where the key is hidden.

Wolf: And is her house the one with the bluebird weathervane and the three potted geraniums in front?

LRRH: Yes, and it is ever such a long way from here.

Wolf: You know, my dear, that this path is the very longest way to go to your Granny's. You want to go up that little hill there *Gestures to rear of center stage.* and around the small pond at the bottom, and then past the field of sunflowers, and turn left at the spotted cow, and there you are! It is much shorter that way.

The Animal Chorus gasps in disbelief, paws to their mouths.

LRRH: Thank you, Mr. Wolf. Let's see, that's up the hill, around the pond, past the sunflowers, and left at the spotted cow. Got it. Goodbye, and thank you. *Exit LRRH to back of stage center and down below stage level.*

Wolf: That's right. Goodbye, goodbye, my dear. That's it. That's the shortcut. Heh, heh, heh.

Animal Chorus: SSSSS! She didn't obey her mother? Maybe she forgot. She should have done what her mother said. I hope she will be all right.

Wolf: That little silly will be at least two hours getting to her Granny's house. I'll rush right over to Granny's house, gobble up the old one, and then wait for Little Red Riding Hood. She'll make a tasty afternoon snack. Heh, heh.

Chorus: Boo! Boo! SSSS! Cad! Villain! Scum! Nasty carnivore!

Wolf: Oh hush, all of you. *Goes to cottage, stage right.*

Wolf: Here we are. Red geraniums, bluebird weathervane, four taps. *knocks four times*

Granny: Yes. Who is it?

Wolf: Falsetto. It is I, Little Red Riding Hood. I've brought you a basket of goodies to make you well.

Granny: Are you sure you are Little Red Riding Hood? She doesn't know the rules of grammar very well, and she usually says "It is me," which is incorrect you know.

Wolf: Oh, well. I have been working very hard at school, and my grammar has improved. I understand all about pronouns now, and I say "It is I," which *is* correct. *To audience.* I think that this Granny used to be a teacher.

Granny: That's lovely, dear. You'll find the key in the first geranium.

Animal Chorus: Gasps. No Granny, no!

Wolf: Enters cottage. Heh, heh. Aha!

The Animal Chorus is silent, hold each other, and lean their heads together. Then they mumbling and whimper.

Granny: Why, you're not Little Red Riding Hood. You are the big bad Wolf. Help, help!

Wolf jumps at Granny and both disappear behind stage right.

Chorus: SSSSSSS! Boo! *Mutterings of anger and growling.*

Wolf: Reappears stage right in Granny's cap. That Granny was certainly thin. Why I just swallowed her whole. She's still wiggling around down there in my tummy. Be quiet in there, Granny. I'm going to have a nap while I wait for Little Red Riding Hood.

Wolf lies down in bed and snores. Enter LRRH stage center and moves toward stage right. Animal Chorus turns attention to LRRH with mutters of worry, anger, and concern.

Animal Chorus: Out of the frying pan and into the fire. Oh Little Red, foolish, foolish Little Red.

LRRH: Panting. I must have misunderstood that wolf's directions. That hill was very high, and the pond was a huge lake, and there was no spotted cow. At last! Here is Granny's house.

Wolf is snoring loudly.

LRRH: Heavens, Granny is snoring so loudly. I hope she will hear my knock . . . oh, the door is open. *enters*

Animal Chorus: No, don't go in there! No, No! Don't go in there! Be careful. Grrrr! Grrrr!

LRRH: Granny, Granny dear. She does not look well. Her skin is sort of gray. Granny?

Wolf: Falsetto. Is that you, Little Red Riding Hood?

LRRH: Yes, Granny. How are you feeling?

Wolf: I am so weak, my dear. Come a little closer to my bed so that we can talk.

Animal Chorus: Don't do it, Little Red. Run while you can.

LRRH: I've brought you some fruit and cake and honey and eggs. Why Granny, what very big eyes you have!

Wolf: All the better to see you with, my dear.

LRRH: Granny, what very large, hairy, pointy ears you have!

Wolf: All the better to hear you with, my dear.

LRRH: And Granny, what very long, sharp, white, huge, scary teeth you have!

Wolf: All the better to eat you with. *Wolf leaps up.*

Animal Chorus: Growling and snarling. Bad bad Wolf!

LRRH screams and disappears below stage level, screaming continually. Wolf appears at same spot, barking. LRRH stops screaming but does not reappear. Wolf reappears stage right.

43

Wolf: Where is she? She got away, but I will find her. Yoo hoo, little girl, where are you?

Animal Chorus: SSSSS!

Woodsman enters center stage and moves to stage right.

Woodsman: What is going on in there? I heard screaming.

Animal Chorus: Yeah. Woo, woo, woo! Hurray! *Cheering, whistling, and woo-woo-ing, then chanting.* Woodsman! Woodsman!

Woodsman: Are you all right, Granny?

Wolf: I'm just fine. You must have heard the television.

LRRH: Appears center stage and approaches Woodsman from behind. It was not. It was me screaming. The Big Bad Wolf is in there, and he tried to eat me up. And my grandmother is nowhere to be seen.

Woodsman: Hits Wolf with mallet. Take that, Wolfie. Now, what have you done with Granny?

Granny: Very muffled from offstage. Help! Help!

Woodsman: What was that?

Granny: Offstage. I said, help, help. Look in the wolf's mouth.

Woodsman: Open up, Wolf. *Looks in.* Why, Granny is inside the wolf. Turn around, Wolf, and I will give you a smart smack between the shoulder blades.

Wolf turns around and Woodsman hits him on the back. Wolf coughs with his mouth below the stage level. Granny pops up from behind stage.

Chorus: Yay, Granny. Yay, Granny.

Granny: Well, I never. It was very warm and cozy inside the wolf. I'm feeling quite well, tip-top. Like going to a spa! Thank you, Wolfie. Why don't you stay here in the cottage with me, and I will make you potato pancakes and jam tarts every day? Once you have eaten one of my jam tarts, you will never want to devour old grannies or little girls again.

Wolf: Okay. If it's all right with Mr. Woodsman.

Woodsman: Yes indeed, but if I hear one little cry from this cottage, it's the zoo for you, Mr. Wolf.

LRRH: Well, what about me? I got all hot and tired and dusty, and my red riding hood is all dirty, and . . .

All: Quiet!

Granny: Young lady, you are to go straight home and you will try to be less vain. Looks aren't everything, you know. And leave the basket.

LRRH: Oh, I'll try. *Sniff.* Goodbye. *Exits stage left.*

Granny: Come on, Wolfie. I have a lovely cushion for you by the fire. Let's see, what is in this basket? *Granny and Wolf exit stage right.*

Woodsman: To audience. Little Red Riding Hood learned her lesson. She tried hard not to be so vain and learned all that she could about pronouns. She never talked to any wolves again, except for her grandmother's pet wolf. They became good friends. And that is the end of our play!

Chorus: Yay, yay, yay! *They bounce up and down with cheers and whistles.* The end! The end!

Playing Notes

Puppeteers and Puppets

Classroom Production

Many children can participate in this play. In addition to having one puppeteer for each character, the Animal Chorus can be as large as you have room and puppets for. Instead of puppets, the chorus can be played by children with painted faces and surround masks. This makes an interesting and appealing variation. The chorus animals may want to compose their own lines. Write the words down, however, so that there is not too much of the unpredictable. Add butterflies and birds made of paper and mounted on flexible rods so that they can flit about when LRRH goes into the forest.

Library Production

Two puppeteers and a helper can put this play on without difficulty. The role of the narrator is taken by one of the minor characters (Mother or Woodsman) and the Animal Chorus is eliminated. One puppeteer is LRRH, Mother, and the Woodsman. The other is the Wolf and the Grandmother. After the Mother has completed her lines, remove her and substitute the Woodsman. The helper assists with puppet changes, holds up the bird and butterfly rods, and puts the granny nightcap on Wolf. There is a shorter version of this script in the appendix.

Props and Scenery

Mother's house is on stage left; Grandmother's house on stage right. Houses are suggested by a piece of furniture placed on the stage, a backdrop, or a two-dimensional cutout of furniture attached to the front of the stage. Granny's house must have a bed, the geraniums, and a bluebird weathervane. Except for the bed, any of these can be eliminated from the script if they pose a problem. Decorate the front of the stage with a woodland scene. A stone pathway wanders through the trees, bushes, rocks, etc. Each of the characters in the Animal Chorus holds a tree or bush that they can hide behind. When all are hiding, they appear to be a forest backdrop.

You can simplify this by having two large, one-piece forest backdrops, placing the chorus between them.

Action

LRRH delivers her lines in an arrogant, whiny voice with a staccato tempo, but not too fast. Mother is excessively patient and long-suffering. Wolf is smooth, sophisticated, clever, and in the end, contrite. Granny is matter-of-fact, and the Woodsman strong. Backstage control is important in this play. Appoint a chorus director who cues and assists the children in the Animal Chorus, which must be placed well behind and slightly above the playing area. They must be careful to speak their lines only when the other characters have finished and vice versa. The greenery they hide behind can be used to rest arms if you use puppets. The flitting birds and butterflies disappear when Wolf enters so that attention is focused on the words again. The flitting, plus some noises from the chorus, accompany LRRH's entrance into the forest and last a few minutes. The chase scene between LRRH and Wolf can last as long as you wish and should be accompanied by lots of screaming, barking, and growling, from LRRH and Wolf.

Program Building

Library Programs

Stories: Tell another familiar tale such as "The Gingerbread Boy." It invites participation and works well in a flannel board set. *Read Aloud:* "The Pig's Picnic." *Music:* Sing "Over the River and Through the Woods" or "Who's Afraid of the Big Bad Wolf." *Short Craft:* Make a simple pop-up cup puppet of LRRH and the Wolf. Have the children practice the infamous litany, "Granny, what big ears you have."

Classroom Study Units

Little Red Riding Hood, with its strong message—"Be yourself or you will fall prey to flatterers and villains"—is very well known and very strong. With its timeless chorus—"Granny, what big eyes you have"—it invites playfulness, invention, and variations. One of the strengths of folk literature is its ability to incorporate change. New variations arise, flourish for a time, and then become part of the story's legacy. Compare this version with others, introducing a discussion of the vital nature of folk literature. Examine some variations of *Little Red Riding Hood* by different authors. Read some of the "fractured fairytale" collections. Collect as many different illustrations as can be found. Have the children illustrate and write their own versions setting the story in locations of their choice—he city or towns here they live—a futuristic, interplanetary world—or among the cowboys of the old West. Briefly explain the concept of a chorus in drama and its place in the theater of Ancient Greece.

Bibliography

Picture Books

Big Anthony and the Magic Ring. Tomie de Paola. Harcourt Brace Jovanovich, 1979. (1–3)
Dandelion. Don Freeman. Viking, 1964. (P–K)
Gingerbread Man. Paul Galdone. Seabury, 1975. (P–K)
Lion. William Pene Du Bois. Viking, 1957. (K–2)
Pigs' Picnic. Keiko Kasza. Putnam, 1988. (P–K)

Longer Fiction

Be a Perfect Person in Three Days! Stephen Manes. Houghton Mifflin, 1982. (4–6)
Sleeping Ugly. Jane Yolen. Putnam, 1981. (2–4)

Versions of Little Red Riding Hood

Armand Eisen, reteller. Knopf, 1988.
Complete Grimm's Fairy Tales. Pantheon, 1972.
Jacob and Wilhelm Grimm, illustrator Trina Schart Hyman. Holiday House, 1983.
James Marshall, reteller and illustrator. Dial, 1987.
Little Red Cap. Lisbeth Zweiger, illustrator. Morrow, 1983.

Paul Galdone, illustrator; McGraw Hill, 1974
Tales Told Again. Walter de la Mare. Faber & Faber, 1973.

Fractured Fairy Tales

Revolting Rhymes. Roaul Dahl. Knopf, 1983. (6–8)
The Stinky Cheese Man and Other Fairly Stupid Tales. Jon Scieszka. Viking, 1992. (3–5)

Stories

"Echo and Narcissus." In *Heroes Gods and Monsters of the Greek Myths.* Four Winds, 1967. (5–8)
The Emperor's New Clothes. Hans Christian Andersen; Anthea Bell, reteller; North South, 1986. (3–4)
The Emperor's New Clothes. Hans Christian Andersen; Janet Stevens, adapter; Holiday House, 1985. (2–4)
Lon Po Po: A Red Riding Hood Story from China. Ed Young. Philomel, 1989. (2–5)

Nonfiction

(See wolf books about wolves with three little pigs)
The Country Artist: A Story About Beatrix Potter. David Collins. Carolrhoda, 1989. (3–5)
Isaac Bashevis Singer: The Story of a Storyteller. Paul Dresh. Lodestar, 1994. (6–8)
Nothing Is Impossible: The Story of Beatrix Potter. Dorothy Aldis. Peter Smith, 1969. (3–6)
Once upon a Time: A Story of the Brothers Grimm. Robert Quackenbush. Prentice Hall, 1985. (3–5)

Songs

"Over the River and Through the Woods." Lydia Childs. Little Brown, 1989. (K–3)
"Teddy Bears Picnic." *Tickle You* (sound recording). R.S. Records. (P–2)
"Who's Afraid of the Big Bad Wolf?" *The Disney Collection* (sound recording). Disneyland Records and Tapes, 1987. (P–3)

5

Maui: Two Legends

Maui Fishes Up the Islands

Maui Ensnares the Sun

Performers: grades 5 through 8
Audience: grades 4 through 6

Cast: Narrator
Maui (foster child of gods)
Tonga-loa, brother
Hemoanauli-uli, brother
Hiku-leo, brother
Mother of Maui

Props: Flames and islands

Set: Waves and Island of Bolotu

Enter Narrator from stage right to center stage.

Narrator: We are going to show to you the story of Maui. They say in the early days the people who lived in the Pacific Islands did not have a barb for their spears. They did not have trap doors for their eel pots. It was Maui, the hero, who brought these things. In the beginning, when the gods lived on the island of Bolotu, the other islands were at the bottom of the sea. The legends say that it was Maui who brought them to the surface. Maui separated the earth from the sky and made the sun go slowly across the sky. Maui learned the secret of fire and brought that secret to the people. When he was born, Maui was small and misshapen, so his mother left him at the edge of the ocean. Maui was adopted by the gods of the ocean and taught wisdom by his ancestors in the sky. When he grew up, Maui decided to return to the earth to find his family.

Narrator moves to far stage left as Maui enters stage right, goes to center stage, and looks back to stage right.

Narrator: Maui came upon his brothers playing a game called riti. There was Tango-loa. *Enters stage left .* Tango-loa threw his spear. *Mimes throwing spear toward audience.* There was Hemoanauli-uli. *Enters stage left.* He threw his spear. *Mimes.* There was Hiku-leo. *Enters stage left.* He threw his spear. *Mimes.* They threw their spears against a rock to see whose spear would bounce the highest. They saw Maui and laughed at him. *Mime.* Maui threw his spear against the rock so hard that the rock shattered into a million pieces. *Maui mimes this and brothers mime surprise. Narrator exits to far stage left.*

Maui: I am Maui, your brother. Come, I will show you how to carve a barb on your spear so that your fish will not fall off when you catch them. After that I will show you how to make a trap door for your eel pots so when you catch eels, they cannot escape.

Tonga-loa: Go away, Maui. We are going fishing.

Hemoanauli-uli: Here is our canoe. *All three mime climbing into canoe at stage center rear.*

Maui: I will come too. *Mimes getting into canoe.*

Brothers: Growl and grunt. Why does he insist on fishing with us? I wish he would go back to the sky to live.

They mime paddling. Maui stops and points stage left.

Maui: Stop! I will fish here. *Mimes throwing out line and pulling it in repeatedly, catching nothing.*

Hiku-leo: Why do you fish here, Maui? There are no fish here.

Maui: I will fish here. *Throws out line again.*

Tonga-loa: He is a fool . . . and ugly too.

Hemoanauli-uli: Ha ha. He doesn't know how to fish.

Hiku-leo: Maui the hero! Ha! Oh, look!

Maui mimes feeling a strong tug and pulling in a heavy weight.

Maui: Help me, help me, brothers.

Tonga-loa: No, no. The fish is so heavy that our canoe will tip over and sink if you try to reel in this giant fish. Let it go!

Hemoanauli-uli: Let go of the line! Let go of the line!

Maui: No! You must help me. You are my brothers! Brother must help brother!

Hiku-leo: We will help. *They help.*
A large land mass arises stage left.

Maui: It is land! It is a fine new island! *Moves to stage right, rear.*
Brothers move to stage left, rear. Narrator enters and goes to center.

Narrator: The great island broke into pieces.

Pieces of island are separated by puppeteers and carried to designated areas on the edges of the playing area. The narrator points to islands as they are named.

Narrator: The biggest island was New Zealand. It is also called Te-ika-a-Maui—the fish that Maui caught. The other islands were Ata, Tonga, Samoa, and Fiji. Papa-langi, Vavau, and Maabai were also brought to the surface of the ocean by Maui. Time passed. Maui noticed that the days were very short. This was the reason. Every day the sun, Tama-nui-a-te-ra came up in the east. *Sun enters far stage right.* Then the sun raced across the sky.

Sun walks very quickly to stage left, makes a turn, lowers head, and goes back to stage right. The head is kept lowered when Sun stops.

Narrator: It took about two hours for the sun to pass across the sky. Imagine—a day that was only two hours long. The people barely got their canoes in the water to fish when the sun set. They made tapa cloth and set it out in the sun to dry, and then the sun would set. The tapa cloth rotted before it dried out. Maui's mother went to him.

Narrator moves to far stage left. Maui moves from rear stage right to center stage front. Maui's mother enters stage right and moves to center stage.

Mother: Maui! The sun moves too quickly for us. There are not enough hours of sunlight for the people to complete their work. We catch no fish to eat. We do not gather fruits. The tapa cloth does not dry. All because the day is too short. Can you help us, Maui? We are hungry!

Maui: I, Maui, will make the sun slow down!

Mother: How can this be done? The sun's heat is terrible. It will burn you.

Maui: You have seen what I can do. I raised great islands from the bottom of the ocean. Give me a net and a club.

Mother mimes giving these to Maui. They move to stage right, Maui to right of Mother.

Maui: Mother, wait until the sun rises, and then help me throw this net over the sun.

Sun: Rises by raising head. It is day. I must run quickly to the other side of the world. Out of my way!

Maui: No you don't! This net will stop you.

Maui and Mother mime throwing net at sun. Sun mimes being caught and struggling. Sun throws flames at Maui and his mother. Maui beats at sun with an imaginary club. Mother continues to hang on to imaginary net ensnaring Sun.

Maui: There and there and there. *Match words with blows.*

Sun: Ow! Ow! Ow! *Throws flames.* Why are you beating me? I am the mighty Sun. What have I done?

Maui: I beat you because you refuse to go slowly across the sky. You must give the people many hours of sunlight to gather their food. They are hungry. You must give them sunlight to do their work. You must give them time to play, too. Slow down!

Sun: I do not care about the people. I will not slow down.

Maui: You will slow down. You will provide light for the people, as much as they need. *They struggle again, club blows and flames.*

Sun: Stop! Stop. You win. I promise I will go slowly across the sky and give the people many hours of light. They will be able to do all their work and play. Please let me go.

The fight stops. Maui and Mother mime removing net from sun.

Maui. There. You may go. Do not forget your promise.

Sun moves slowly across the stage, halting now and then to look back at Maui, who uses a gesture to urge it forward. Sun reaches other side of stage and lowers head.

Mother: Now there will be time to fish and dry tapa cloth.

Maui: Now there will be time to play.

Narrator: Moves to stage center. There were other things which Maui did for the people. There are many stories about Maui that tell of his adventures. Ask to hear them, listen well, and tell those stories to others. Our play is ended. The end.

All puppets move to center and bow.

Playing Notes

Puppeteers and Puppets

Classroom Production

To include more children, divide the Narrator's lines among two or three children. The narrator dresses in dark colors and may wear a dark mask or hood on the head. If you want to make more puppets, the narrators can carry a full-sized puppet and speak through the puppet. The puppets are giant puppets with two or even three puppeteers to manipulate the head and each arm. Simplify the production by making large masks rather than puppets. The island pieces are raised up, carried to their location, and held by students dressed in dark clothes and wearing hoods or simple masks. It is important for the puppeteers and helpers to be dressed in the same dark clothing and to wear a mask or hood. The ocean waves are moved by two or four children.

Library Production

Use masks rather than puppets for library production. You must have at least three—Maui, a brother, and the sun—to perform this play. The sun performs the narrator's lines, moving to center stage to do so. Tongo-loa takes all the brothers' and the mother's lines. Change some of the mother's lines to begin "Our mother has said . . ." Other lines will seem as appropriate to a brother as to the mother. There is a shorter version of this script in the appendix.

Puppets

Ovals are cut of cardboard, tag board, poster board, or foam core. You will need one oval for each character, eighteen inches across and twenty-four inches long. Create faces on the circles with paint or colored paper glued to a circle. To make a movable mouth, cut two rectangular pieces of card stock or foam core. One piece measures two inches by three inches. The other is three inches by three inches. Cut the narrower piece into the shape of an upper lip. Cut the other piece into the shape of a chin and lower lip. Glue the upper lip to the face. Attach a brass

fastener to the face two inches below the center of the upper lip. Attach brass fasteners to the right and left sides of the lower lip and to the center of the chin near the lower edge. Slip a rubber band over the legs of the fasteners on the lower lip so that it hangs between them. Then slip the rubber band over the fastener attached to the face behind the head of the fastener. You might want to add a bit of tape. Tie a length of strong buttonhole thread to the fastener on the chin. The puppeteer holding the head wraps the thread around his or her index finger. Pulling down on the thread will make the mouth open. When the thread is released, the rubber band will pull the mouth closed. Make puppet hair out of black crepe paper streamers. Attach it to the head so that some falls forward over the face as well as behind. The mother's hair must be about three feet long. Add a flower crown to the mother's hair.

Two dowels are needed for the body: one one inch in diameter and four feet long, and the other one-half inch in diameter and four feet long. Mark the one-inch dowel at ten inches and at fifteen inches. Using four four-inch strips of duct tape, attach the half-inch dowel to the one-inch dowel at the fifteen-inch mark, making a cross. Attach the tape in a series of "X" patterns. Attach the head to the one-inch dowel with the chin at the ten-inch mark.

The cross piece will form the puppet's shoulders. To the shoulders, attach many crepe paper streamers, six to eight feet long, to form the arms and body of the puppet. Some of the streamers are gathered into sections and bound together to form the arms. Let the body streamers hang and flow with the movement. Use brightly colored streamers to suggest clothing, and cut hands out of tan paper. Maui, because he is related to the ocean, is made from ocean colors. Make the sun from orange, yellow, and red streamers. A rod is attached to each of the hands. Quarter-inch dowels cut into two one-foot lengths work well. If one puppeteer is manipulating both hands, experiment with the length of the rods until the action is comfortable. Maui should be larger than his brothers. If you are not making all the brother puppets, place small (three-inch) paper cutout figures along the shoulders of the brother puppet to represent Maui's family and his people. Make sure the puppets do not get too heavy.

Props and Scenery

This play is not produced on a conventional puppet theater. A stage or floor area that is at least twenty feet square is necessary. Delineate the front of the "stage" with a rope that is stretched horizontally across the playing area at about a two-foot level. White, green, and blue streamers hang from this rope to simulate the ocean. Two lines of ocean "waves" are held at each end by one or two children. Move the cords in a horizontal, rocking motion that makes the ocean appear to move in waves. Using a theater-in-the-round arrangement, have waves on all sides. Make the islands from pieces of poster board painted brown and green. The island of Bolutu is represented by a backdrop or a ladder draped in green sheeting. The flames are orange and yellow streamers attached to a small ball, an eraser, or something to weight them. Helpers throw the flames.

Action

The puppeteer carrying the head leads the hand puppeteers and determines the direction and speed of movement. The movement of the puppets must be practiced many times. The sun must practice moving quickly across the playing area and back to the beginning point. The puppeteers must practice walking, entering a canoe, paddling, throwing a fishing line, pulling in a fishing line for Maui and the brothers, handing over objects, holding on to a net, and fighting and clubbing. The Sun must also practice walking quickly, struggling in a net, and throwing flames.

Program Building

Library Productions

Stories: Learn and tell another story from Polynesian folk literature. *Read Aloud:* "The Three Little Hawaiian Pigs and the Magic Shark," "The Fire Children," or "Max and Ruby's First Greek Myth." *Music:* Play a tape of Polynesian music while audience is being seated. Learn a Hawaiian dance and teach it to the children. *Short Craft:* Make flower leis or crowns with flowers cut from colored paper and glued to strips of paper cut long enough to circle a child's head or neck.

Classroom Study Units

Along with the richness of the folk literature, the animal life, plant life, and history of the Pacific Islands all provide a wealth of exciting material for classroom units. Create study centers for each of these areas in the classrooms. The overall geography and the dramatic weather patterns of the area should be included also. Plan and take an imaginary voyage to the Pacific Islands on a sailing ship. Begin your journey in New York. Assemble all the provisions and the crew for a voyage that will take many months. Have each student keep a log of the life aboard ship. Plan and hold a luau.

Bibliography

Picture Books

A is for Aloha. Stephanie Feeney. University Press of Hawaii, 1980. (P–K)
Dumpling Soup. Jane Kim Rattigan. Little, Brown, 1993. (P–K)
I Visit my Tutu and Grandma. Nancy Mower. Press Pacifica, 1984. (K–2)
In the Night, Still Dark. Richard Leis. Atheneum, 1988. (K–2)
Luka's Quilt. Georgia Guback. Greenwillow Books, 1994. (1–3)
Max and Ruby's First Greek Myth: Pandora's Box. Rosemary Welles. Dial, 1993. (P–1)
Song to Demeter. Cynthia and William Birrer. Lothrop, 1987. (K–2)
The Three Little Hawaiian Pigs and the Magic Shark. Donivee Laird. Bess Press, 1981. (K–2)
To Find a Way. Susan Nunes. University Press of Hawaii, 1992.
Why There Is no Arguing in Heaven: A Mayan Myth. Deborah Nourse Lattimore. Harper and Row, 1989. (2–6)

Longer Fiction

Aloha: A Novel. Mark Christiansen. Simon & Schuster, 1994. (4–6)
Blue Skin of the Sea. Graham Salisbury. Delacorte, 1992. (5–8)

The Broccoli Tapes. Jan Slepian. Philomel, 1989. (4–6)

Pearl Harbor Is Burning. Kathleen V. Kudlinski. Viking, 1991. (4–6)

Shark Dialogues. Kiana Davenport. Maxwell Macmillan, 1994. (5–8)

Surfboard to Peril: A Miss Mallard Mystery. Robert Quackenbush. Prentice-Hall, 1986. (3–4)

Who Did It, Jenny Lake? Jean Davies Okimoto. Putnam, 1983. (4–6)

Stories

Backbone of the King: The Story of Paka'a and his Sonku. Marcia Brown. University Press of Hawaii, 1984. (P–3)

The Dark Way. Virginia Hamilton. Harcourt Brace Jovanovich, 1990. (5–8)

How Maui Slowed the Sun. Suelyn Ching Tune. University Press of Hawaii, 1988. (P–3)

The Surprising Things Maui Did. Jay Williams. Four Winds Press, 1980. (P–3)

Nonfiction

Hawaii Is a Rainbow. Stephanie Feeney. University of Hawaii, 1985. (2–6)

Haleakala National Park. Ruth Radlauer. Children's Press, 1979. (3–5)

The Last Princess: The Story of Princess Ka'iulani of Hawai'i. Fay Stanley. Four Winds Press, 1991. (3–6)

Hawaii: The Aloha State. Helen Bauer. Bess Press, 1982. (4–7)

The Hawaiians: An Island People. Helen Jay Pratt. Tuttle, 1963. (6–8)

Hawaii. Sylvia McNair. Children's Press, 1989. (6–8)

Music

Hawaiian Rainbow Music (sound recording). Rounder, 1988.

6

The Princess And The Pea

Performers: grades 3 through 6
Audience: grades preschool through grade 3

Cast: Narrator
Queen Beatrice
Prince Chester
Princess Jane of Backgammon Board
Giles, a servant
Lady in Waiting

Props: Bed, ladder, book *(The Princess Directory).* rain slicker and hat for Princess Jane over a very long nightgown.

Set: Castle.

Narrator: A long time ago, royalty was kind of important. Princes and princesses and kings and queens thought it was necessary for them and their children to marry someone who was royal as well. But in fairy stories and folk tales everyone knew that what really mattered was to be kind and honest. Being beautiful or handsome didn't hurt, either. *The Princess and the Pea* is about a very silly queen who didn't know what was important or good or even useful or fun. She was so silly that she and this story have become quite famous.

Exit Narrator. Prince Chester enters stage right and looks out an imaginary window toward the audience. There is the sound of wind and rain and thunder outside. Queen Beatrice enters stage left.

Queen: Good evening, Chester dear.

Chester: Good evening, Mother. The storm is very wild. Did you hear the thunder? The moat will be very full with all this rain.

Queen: Never mind the moat, dear. Come away from the window. You and I must have a very, very important talk.

Chester: Oh dear. Is it about my suit of armor? I have told you, Mother, that I will not wear it. It's hot, and noisy, and it scares people.

Queen. No, no, no, it's not about the armor, although I must say you do look very royal and princely in it. I have decided that it is time that you were married. We must find a suitable wife for you.

Chester: Oh! All right! I'd like to marry someone who has a nice voice and likes to sing songs about mountains and fields. And someone who is strong and likes to hike, and . . .

Queen: Stuff and nonsense! None of that is of any consequence, my dear. What really matters in the royal world is that your wife must be of royal blood. You must marry a princess. You cannot marry just any young lady you like. She must have a king for a papa, and a queen for a mama. She must have a crown and live in a castle with a moat and a dungeon and at least two thrones.

Chester: But I would like a wife who likes to read and hike and search for wild mushrooms. Let's try to find a princess who likes to do those things.

Queen: Be serious, son. Princesses like making lace, and listening to mechanical birds, and drinking chamomile tea. So you and I must look up suitable princesses in this *Princess Directory. Aside.* I borrowed this one from the . . . Library. *Leans over so hands are below stage level and stands up with large book.* Come along dear. *They move to center stage.*

Chester: This is going to be very difficult, I'm afraid. Now, Mother, you know that your happiness is very important to me, but you also know that I . . .

Loud banging is heard.

Jane: Offstage. Help, help. Please let us in, oh please let us in.

Queen: Why, whoever could that be on such a stormy night? Probably some commoner looking for something common. Giles!

Enter Giles, a servant, stage left.

Giles: Yes, Your Highness.

Queen: Giles, someone is banging at the palace door. Go see who it is and send them away.

Giles bows and exits stage right.

Queen: Aside. You boys and girls must think I am a terrible snob, but really what is a mother to do? Chester must marry a princess, and he's not very clever, and besides, that is the way the story goes, so pish posh.

Giles returns with Jane and lady-in-waiting, stage right.

Giles: Your Highness, this is the Princess Jane of Backgammon Board. *Giles backs up to center stage rear.*

Queen: Oh! Well then, I am Her Royal Highness Queen Beatrice. This is my son, Prince Chester.

Jane: Your majesties! *Curtsies.* Please forgive me for this intrusion. I am so very sorry to arrive uninvited, and in this condition. Truly, I am quite desperate. I was out in the forest pursuing my study of mycology when the storm began, and I lost my way. I have been through brambles and swamps, and I fell into your moat. Please permit me to take shelter here. And would you please please send someone to look after my lady-in-waiting.

Lady: Atchoo, atchoo, atchoo. Cough, cough, sniff.

Jane: I think that she might have caught cold.

Queen: Hmmm! The Princess of Backgammon Board. Hmmm. And what does your father do, my dear?

Jane: Why nothing! He is a king, you know.

Queen: Of course. Well, we'll see. Now you must get out of those wet clothes and have a hot bath and some hot chocolate. I will show you where the royal bathroom is, and I will send a maid with dry clothes and warm towels. We will fix some hot herbal tea for your lady. In the meantime, I will have a cozy bed prepared for you.

Jane: I am most grateful. You see, I am quite exhausted.

Chester: Ah, Princess, did you say that your hobby was mycology, the study of fungi?

Jane: Why, yes. Are you interested in fungi also?

Chester: Indeed I am. Passionately so. Have you ever found a *morchessa esculenta*?

Queen: Chester! The Princess is cold and wet!

Chester: Oh, yes. Sorry. Come right this way, Princess.

Chester and Princess exit stage left.

Queen: I wonder. She could be a real princess, you know. Probably she is, but we must be absolutely certain of it. We will just have to give her the princess test. Now, a real princess has very very sensitive skin. When she is in her royal bed, the smallest lump in the mattress, the smallest wrinkle in the sheets, will make her miserable and keep her awake all night. I will have a bed made up for her with a little, hard, dry green pea in it. If she can feel that pea through the mattress, perhaps two mattresses, then we will know that she is a real princess. Giles!

Giles: Jumps. Yes, Your Highness.

Queen: Go to the royal basement and get the princess testing bed and move it into this room.

Giles: Yes, madam. *Bows and exits stage right.*

Queen: Calls after him. And hurry!

Sounds of banging, thumping, and grunting, cries of pain and sighs. Queen glances offstage and looks at audience alternately.
Queen: My Goodness! *Looks at bed.* Heavens! *Looks.* Wow! *Looks.*

Giles enters stage right, pushing bed up and across to far stage left with much difficulty. The bed tilts wildly, toward the Queen, toward the audience, and toward Giles, threatening to crush him. Giles and Queen respond with cries of alarm, fear, and warning. Queen moves back and forth, watching and putting her hands to her mouth and face and tilting her head to indicate involvement.

Giles: Panting. There you are, Your Highness. *Giles collapses over edge of stage.*

Queen: Pushes Giles's body sideways all the way to edge of stage right where it slips down out of view behind stage. There. Now, I wonder if that's enough mattresses. Let's see: one, two, three, four . . . Well, it will have to do. Now, I will put the tiny little pea under the bottom mattress. *Mimes doing this.* There we are. *Exits and returns with ladder, placing it stage right leaning against stage support or scenery.* A ladder for her to climb into the bed completes the plot. Now, if she is a princess, that pea will feel like a mountain to her. Ah, here she is. Don't tell her about the pea. Shhh!

Enter Jane stage right in a very long nightgown and crown.

Jane: Thank you for your kindness, Queen Beatrice. My lady-in-waiting has had some tea and hot soup, and I am quite dry and warm.

Queen: Very good, my dear. You look much more comfortable now. I expect you are also quite tired and ready for sleep. I have prepared a very soft bed for you. There you are.

Jane: Heavens. How high it is! *Leans backward very far as she looks at the bed.* Thank you, Your Majesty. I am so tired from wandering in the storm that I think I could sleep on a rock tonight. *Yawns.*

Queen: Good night, Princess Jane. Sleep well. *Exits stage right.*

Jane: Dear me, how am I going to get into that bed. Oh well, up I go. *Jane tries to get into to bed from the foot of the bed, grunting, and slips down.* OOOO! Oh, dear. *Studies bed.* Maybe if I got a run at it. *She tries running at the bed from stage right.* Hiii Ahhh! *Flings herself at bed, hesitates, and slips down.* I do believe I am making some progress. I will try beginning my run a little further away and faster. *Goes all the way to far stage right.* Hiii Ahhhh!

Jane flings herself at bed as before and slips down—all ladylike of course. The bed sways and rocks and tilts. This can go on as long as audience appreciates it.

Jane: Oh dear. How am I going to get into that bed? Do you boys and girls have any ideas? What? A ladder. Oh. Do you see a ladder anywhere? What? Oh my. *Laughs and gets ladder from stage right.* Wish I'd found this before I did all that jumping and climbing. *Puts ladder on side of bed away from audience and gets onto bed.*

Jane: There. I am utterly worn out. *Sighs then snores.* Ow! A lump, a great big lump. Perhaps if I move over here. *Snores.* Oh. No. Maybe on my side. *Snore.* No, oh no.

Flops, groans, and moans, and at last falls out of bed. The bed sways wildly and it falls over with a crash behind stage. Queen and Chester enter stage right. Jane pulls herself to stage level and then stands, stage left. The bed is gone.

Queen: Princess Jane! What happened?

Chester: We heard a loud crash. Are you all right?

Jane: Oh dear, Oh my, I am so embarrassed. You see, there was a great lump in the bed, and I could not get comfortably settled. And in my efforts to discover a comfortable position and fall asleep, I fell out of bed and knocked the bed over, too. I am so terribly, terribly sorry. *Hands to face, she turns from Queen to Chester and back to indicate distress.*

Queen: Aside. She is a real princess! *To Jane.* No need to apologize, my dear. No need at all. Come with me, and I will find a bed worthy of a princess. Your royal sleep will not be disturbed again.

Jane: Thank you. You have been so very kind. *Jane and Queen exit stage left.*

Chester: Well, boys and girls. This is going quite well. I like that Princess Jane a lot. True, she was a little stupid about the ladder, but nobody is perfect. I think that the Princess likes me too. And she likes hiking and mushroom hunting too. My silly mother is quite satisfied that she is a real princess. And while I don't care at all about that, it's nice that Mother's happy. I sent Giles on a two-week vacation in the south of France and he is recovering nicely. Soon Jane's mother and father and my mother and father will get together and do lots of talking about whether Jane and I should marry. I do believe that it is very likely that when all the talking is done, we will get married and live happily ever after. The end.

Playing Notes

Puppeteers and Puppets

Classroom Production

Include many children in this play by adding an introductory song to set the mood. A puppet chorus dressed in royal costume sings "Greensleeves" or some other song for the amusement of Queen Beatrice and Prince Chester. Include a conductor who uses extravagant gestures. Have one puppeteer per character. Add another servant to help Giles with the bed. Add dog puppets to bark at the knocking on the door and harass Giles as he is moving the bed. Appoint a sound crew to make the sounds of the storm, the movement and fall of the bed, and Jane's running. A puppet with a lute may be added to sing Jane a lullaby. Jane orders him from the room as her struggle with the bed grows more intense.

Library Productions

This play can be performed easily by two puppeteers and a helper if the parts of the lady-in-waiting and Giles are eliminated. Without Giles, the Queen moves the bed herself and this can be very funny in itself. One puppeteer is the Queen and Chester; the other is Jane and the bed. The lady-in-waiting is kept as an offstage voice. The business with the bed is carried on as long as the audience enjoys it and the puppeteer's strength holds out.

Props and Scenery

The bed is a very important prop and is almost a puppet itself. Mount a four-inch by eight-inch piece of sturdy cardboard or foam core on a half-inch dowel six inches long to create a platform. Make the mattresses by stitching five or six pieces of foam inside pillowcases made of fabrics of different colors and patterns. Stitch all the mattresses together in several places with long, loose stitches that run vertically through all of the mattresses. You want the mattresses to move a little. Glue the bottom mattresses to the platform. Add a fancy bedskirt to the platform to hide the puppeteer's hand and to make the bed more suitable for a princess. Make sure that the bed is sturdy; it will have to withstand many shocks as the princess tries to climb it and flings herself about on it. Before the final performances, check the long stitches holding the stack of mattresses together, as they may have been damaged in rehearsal. Decorate the front of the stage with castles, knights and ladies, formal gardens, flags and banners. Use velvet draperies secured with golden cords to decorate the playing area.

Action

The bed must tilt and lean toward the Queen and Jane, and toward the audience as well. The pillows and mattresses must appear to be so loosely attached that they are about to fall off of the bed as it tilts and as Jane struggles. The audience will love this leaning, precarious, ridiculous bed.

The Queen is stuffy and pompous and a comic figure rather than a regal one. Princess Jane is wearing her nightgown and crown under a rain poncho and hood. The poncho has leaves and vines stuck to it; some of them are on the hood and fall over her face. Remove the poncho before Jane reappears in her nightgown. The nightgown must be very long to cover the puppeteer's hand when Jane struggles with the bed. Jane's movements are elegant, her hands moving more than her body. However, she becomes quite athletic as she attempts to get into bed. Her voice remains prissy, however, except when she does her samurai yell as she runs toward the bed. The contrast with her movement is, we hope, funny. Chester, a romantic dreamy prince, looks over the edge of the stage and downward to suggest a window. Giles is slow and a little whiny.

Children can make the sound of the storm by whistling, sprinkling uncooked rice onto a cookie sheet, and shaking a sheet of tin very hard. Records and tapes of storms are readily available also. Many books on theater have suggestions for sound effects. Be sure to explain what a dried pea is when you introduce the play. Show the children what one is. Make copies of a simple recipe for split pea soup and hand them out as the audience leaves.

Chapter 6

Program Building

Library Programs

Stories: Tell another traditional Princess story such as "Snow White," or "Cinderella." *Read Aloud:* "Tough Princess" or a story from *The Stinky Cheese Man. Short Craft:* Make and decorate paper crowns. *Music:* Play a tape of Elizabethan music as the audience gathers. *Other:* Hand out recipes for split pea soup.

Classroom Study Units

Use this play as part of a unit on the medieval period in English history. Include a study of castles, society, dress, everyday life, community life, and warfare. For art projects, read David Macaulay's *Castle* and make castles from papier-mâché, clay, boxes, found objects, etc. Plan a medieval feast, and if your budget can stand it, have one. Use the potluck method and substitute more ordinary foods for some of the unusual ones. Dress in medieval costume and play medieval music. Teach a simple courtly line dance. Have a mock tournament with sponge rubber or polystyrene weapons.

Bibliography

Picture Books

The Frog Prince Continued. Jon Scieszka. Viking, 1991. (3–5)

Prince Boghole. Erik Haugaard. Macmillan, 1987. (3–5)

Princess Smartypants. Babette Cole. Putnam, 1987. (2–4)

The Stinky Cheese Man and Other Fairly Stupid Tales. Jon Scieszka. Viking, 1992. (2–4)

The Tough Princess. Martin Waddle. Philomel, 1987. (2–4)

Longer Books

The 500 Hats of Bartholomew Cubbins. Dr. Seuss. Vanguard, 1938. (2–4)

The Light Princess. George MacDonald. Farrar, Straus and Giroux, 1969. (4–6)

Many Moons. James Thurber. Harcourt Brace, 1943. (2–4)

Mufaro's Beautiful Daughters. John Steptoe. Lothrop, 1987. (1–3)

The Whipping Boy. Sid Fleischmann. Greenwillow, 1986. (3–5)

Nonfiction

The Amazing Paper Cuttings of Hans Christian Andersen. Beth Wagner Brust. Ticknor and Fields, 1991. (4–6)

Castle. David Macaulay. Houghton Mifflin, 1977. (3–6)

Hans Christian Andersen: Prince of Storytellers. Carol Green. Children's Press, 1991. (3–5)

A Medieval Feast. Aliki. Crowell, 1983. (3–5)

Merry Ever After: The Story of Two Medieval Weddings. Joc Lasker. Penguin, 1976. (3–5)

The Middle Ages. Giovanni Caselli. Bedricks, 1988. (4–6)

Sir Dana: A Knight, as Told by his Trusty Armor. Dana Fradon. Dutton, 1988. (3–6)

Songs and Poems

"The Grand Old Duke of York." (Many collections and editions).

"Greensleeves." *A Winter's Solstice.* Windham Hill, 1985.

"Old King Cole." (Many collections and editions).

"Some Day my Prince Will Come." *The New Illustrated Disney Songbook.*

Stories

"Cap O'Rushes." In *Womenfolk and Fairy Tales.* Rosemary Minard. Houghton Mifflin, 1975. (3–6)

Cinderella. Nonny Hogrogian, reteller. Greenwillow, 1981. (1–3)

Snow White and the Seven Dwarves. Macmillan, 1981. (1–3)

Tam Lin. Susan Cooper. Margaret McElderry Books, 1991. (3–6)

The Twelve Dancing Princesses and Other Tales from Grimm. Dial, 1986. (3–6)

7

Rabbit and Hyena Play the Sanza

Performers: grades 4 through 6
Audience: grades 1 through 3
Cast: Narrator
     Rabbit
     Hyena
     Guinea
     Hens (at least three)

Props: Sweet potato, macaroni and cheese mix box, apple core, two cages—one larger and more crude than the other, a pail of "water" (silver or blue confetti), broom, and thumb piano.

Set: A clearing in a forest with a tree at far stage right and another at far left.

Narrator: Enters stage left. Our puppet play is based on a story from Zaire, a country in Africa. The play is called *Rabbit and Hyena Play the Sanza.* The sanza is a musical instrument that looks like this. *Show a sanza.* Sometimes it is called a thumb piano. Sometimes it is called a mbira or a kalimba. Now when our play begins, the animals have all run out of food. It has not rained in a long time, and the animals can barely find enough to eat. All except Rabbit. Rabbit is so clever that he can find food anytime. Well, even Rabbit's food supply was getting low, and he was getting a little worried.

Narrator exits stage left. Rabbit enters stage right and looks behind tree and examines something out of sight and slightly below stage level.

Rabbit: Let's see what I have to eat. Hmmm. Sweet potatoes, instant macaroni and cheese, an apple core. *These items are tossed from below stage right across center stage and fall behind stage left.* What boring food! No marinated artichoke hearts, not one Norwegian sardine, no pesto sauce. I can't be a jumpy rabbit on that stuff. *Returns to stage right front.* I need something fresh and tasty, and fast. *Paces.* Got it! Guinea hens! Yummy and easy to catch.

Rabbit exits stage right and returns pushing a cage before him to center stage. Exits again and returns with a pail and a broom.

Rabbit: There. Now, just get this C-A-G-E over to where it belongs. *Pushes it to far stage left.* Whew. *To audience.* Now, C-A-G-E spells cage. But, that's a secret. Remember, a secret. I'll go get my sanza.

Rabbit exits stage right and returns with sanza. Stands near pail and broom and begins to play.

Rabbit: Hum, hum, hum-hum-hum. *Singing and playing.* "Come one, come all, come dance to the music of my sanza. Come one, come all, come dance to the music of my sanza. The sun is warm, the air is sweet. Come dance, come dance."

The Guinea Hens all enter stage left. They spin, bow, and hop in time to the music.
Guinea Hen: Panting. Rabbit, why are you playing the sanza for us?

Rabbit: Oh, well. It's been such a hard time lately. Not enough food, no rain. I thought you needed cheering up.

Guinea Hen: How kind! Isn't he kind? *To others, they nod.* Thank you, Rabbit!

Rabbit: Think nothing of it.

Guinea Hen: Why do you have that pail of water?

Rabbit: This pail of water? Oh! You see, I get very thirsty when I dance, and I thought maybe you might get thirsty too! So, I have water ready for you to drink.

Guinea Hen: That's true, that's true. Very thoughtful, Rabbit. Very thoughtful indeed. *To others, they nod.* Thank you.

Guinea Hen: Ah, Rabbit. Isn't that a broom? Why do you have a broom?

Rabbit: Yes, well. As you know, you do stir up a lot of dust when you dance, now don't you? And we would not want your beautiful feathers to get dirty, would we? So, between the dances I will sweep up the dust so it won't get on your feathers.

Guinea Hen: I am astonished! What kindness? What thoughtfulness! What—ah—wonderfulness! You are truly a most generous rabbit. *Other Hens notice cage, react with fear, and point it out to speaking Hen.*

Guinea Hen: Gasp! Oooh! Rabbit! That is a cage. Why do you have a cage?

Rabbit: A cage? I do not have a cage. Oh that, ha ha, you thought that was a cage? How amusing. That is a shelter! You know that we are expecting the rainy season to begin any day now. I made that shelter so that if it should begin to rain while you are dancing, you can run into the shelter and keep dry. *Cocks his head to one side.*

Guinea Hen: I see. Yes, of course. That makes sense. Again, we thank you. *All Hens bow.* Now, let's dance!

Rabbit: "Come one, come all. Come dance to the music of my sanza. Come one, come all. Come dance to the music of my sanza. The sun is warm, the air is sweet. Come dance, come dance. The sun is warm, the air is sweet. Come dance, come dance!"

While singing, Rabbit appears to dip broom in pall and sprinkle water over the Hens several times.

Guinea Hen: What was that? I thought I felt a drop of water!

Rabbit: Rain! It's raining. It's raining. Yay, rain! Into the shelter everyone! Into the shelter, into the shelter. Don't let your feathers get wet. Into the shelter, into the shelter!

Guinea Hens: Enter cage. Hurry, hurry, we must not get wet! Hurry! Why, this shelter is very comfortable.

Rabbit: There we are. *Closes door, drops broom and pail below stage.*

Guinea Hen: What are you doing? Why are you closing the door? Let us out! Help! Help! It is a cage! It is a cage! *Sad clucking from all Guinea Hens.*

Hyena: Enters stage right. Hey there, Rabbit. What are you up to?

Rabbit: Just catching me some dinner, and lunch, and breakfast. *Starts to push cage off stage left.* Say, Hyena, give me a hand, would you? I want to store this food away.

Hyena: Sure, Rabbit. Where did you get these birds anyway? I sure would like some.

Rabbit: It was just a little trick I tried—and it worked!

Hyena: If I help you store your food away, will you teach me the trick?

Rabbit: Sure.

They both push cage off stage left with much grunting and groaning. Rabbit enters stage left with Hyena.

Rabbit: Now. To catch these birds you need four things. Number one is a broom!

Hyena: Broom. Right. *Reaches below center stage and brings up broom.*

Rabbit: A pail!

Hyena: One pail coming up. *Reaches below center stage and brings up a pail.*

Rabbit: Looks into pail. Ah, it should have water in it.

Hyena: Oh. Sorry.

Hyena takes pail below stage. Sound of water running goes on for a long time. Rabbit glances below, back at audience, below, back at audience. At last Hyena returns grunting and straining with a very full bucket.

Rabbit: I guess that's enough water. Now you need a cage.

Hyena: A cage. Right. Nice big one. *Goes below stage and returns grunting and straining with a large rickety-looking cage.* How about this, Rabbit? Big enough?

Rabbit: Oh sure. Here, let's push it into place. *They move cage into far left corner.*

Rabbit: Now Hyena, the last and most important thing you need is a sanza.

Hyena: One sanza, coming up. *Goes below center stage and returns with sanza.* There.

Rabbit: Now, you're ready. This is how the trick works. You stand there and play the sanza and sing this song. "Come one, come all. Come dance to the music of my sanza. Come one, come all. Come dance to the music of my sanza. The sun is warm, the air is sweet. Come dance, come dance."

Hyena: Okay. How's this? *Hyena sings in a high, cracking, reedy voice.* "Come one, come all. Come dance to the music of my sanza. Come one, come all. Come dance to the music of my sanza."

Rabbit: Cutting him off. Great! That was really great, Hyena. Don't practice anymore. You are perfect. *Shakes his head to one side as if to shake something out of his ear.* Now, the Guinea Hens will love this song. Trust me. They will come out of the bushes and begin to dance. They will stop and ask you why you are playing the sanza. Then you tell them that you want to cheer them up. They will ask you about the broom, the pail, and the cage. You tell them the broom is to sweep the ground so their feathers won't get dusty.

Hyena: Mimes sweeping. Sweeping.

Rabbit: The pail of water is in case they get thirsty. And the cage is not a cage, but a shelter to protect them from the rain. That is a very important part. The cage is not a cage; it is a shelter. Then, while they are dancing, you dip the broom into the pail, sprinkle the water over the birds and yell: "It's raining, it's raining. Into the shelter, into the shelter."

Hyena: Mimes dipping and sprinkling. "It's raining, it's raining! Into the cage—oops—I mean into the shelter, into the shelter!

Rabbit: Great, Hyena. You've got it. I'm going to go whip up a little mango sauce to go with my dinner. Good luck! *Exits stage right.*

Hyena: Thanks, Rabbit! All right! Now for some trickery. Bring on the Guinea Hens. "Come one, come all. Come dance. Uh, there's the sun, there's the air, come dance!

Guinea Hens enter stage left and dance as before.

Hyena: Louder. "Come dance, come dance. In the sun, it isn't raining. Come dance."

Guinea Hen: Hyena, why are you playing the sanza for us, hmmm?

Hyena: Well, there isn't much food around, and I have to eat too!

Guinea Hen: Oh. I see! *Hens put heads together and cluck.*

Guinea Hen: Hyena, why do you have a pail and a broom?

Hyena: You stupid birds! Don't you realize that they are part of the trick? You will dance some more, and then I will take the broom and dip it into the pail and sprinkle water on your backs. I will say, "It's raining, it's raining. Into the cage—I mean shelter. Into the shelter." Don't you understand?

Guinea Hen: Oh. Yes, we understand.

Hyena: Fine. Now let's dance. "Come and dance while you have a chance. I don't play the sanza every day."

Guinea Hens cluck together but do not dance.

Hyena: What are you doing, you silly creatures? Don't you remember? You're supposed to dance, and then I sprinkle water on you, and yell: "It's raining, it's raining." Then you run into the cage—I mean shelter. *To audience.* I always get that part wrong. *To Hens.* You run into the shelter. Got it?

Guinea Hen: But we have a problem, Hyena. We are silly creatures, you see, and we don't know how to get into that kind of a shelter. Can you show us how?

Hyena: Of, all the stupid birds in the world, you are the most stupid. Look. You just duck your head down, like this, and walk in. *Hyena demonstrates by ducking head down and putting head into cage.*

Guinea Hen: Oh, we know how to duck our heads and get the front part of us in. We just don't know how to get the back part in. How do we get the back parts and tails into the shelter?

Hyena: Oh for pity's sake! Silly creatures. Like this, this is how you get your tails into the shelter. *Hyena enters cage and Guinea Hens slam door shut.*

Hyena: Oh dear. I got it wrong after all. "Come and dance, while you have a chance, to see a Hyena in a cage. Come and dance, while you have a chance, to see a Hyena in a cage."

Guinea hens laugh and dance. Rabbit enters stage right.

Rabbit: The end, the end!

Playing Notes

Puppets and Puppeteers

Classroom Production

Use one puppeteer for each character, including the narrator. To involve more children, make the flock of Guinea Hens larger, and have two flocks, one for Rabbit and one for Hyena. Rod puppets would work very well for the Guinea Hens. You may use different kinds of birds if you wish, but guinea hens are known for their silliness. You will need two students to handle the props. A third person will be necessary to play the sanza. If possible, amplify the sanza music, as it does not make a big sound.

Library Production

Two puppeteers and a helper can perform this play. One puppeteer is Rabbit and the speaking Guinea Hen. The other puppeteer is the Hyena and one of the nonspeaking Guinea Hens. The helper manipulates the props and the other nonspeaking Guinea Hen. Put the sanza music on a tape. The helper must raise and lower the volume.

Scenery and Props

Decorate the front of the stage with African images, animals, masks, plants. The trees at stage left and stage right should not take up too much room, but simply frame the action. Rabbit's sweet potato, macaroni and cheese, and apple core could be the real thing. Use a small sweet potato. Make the pail out of a paper cup covered with foil. Mount it on a small dowel that is held by the prop handler or helper. The "water" (silver or blue confetti or bits of paper) is not in the pail at all. Simply toss it into the air when the puppets sprinkle water.

The broom must have a small piece of Velcro on the handle that will attach it to a small piece on the Rabbit and the Hyena's paw. The sanza also attaches to the paws of the puppets with a bit of Velcro. Make the broom and sanza out of cardboard painted or covered with felt.

The cages are two-dimensional, with no bottom or top. They can be made from painted or felt-covered cardboard. Hinge the door with a brad on the lower front edge. Place another brad on the upper front edge and the top edge of the door. The prop handler closes the door by pulling on a string that is attached to the top edge of the door and the upper brad. It hangs from the upper brad to below stage level.

Action

Rabbit is very clever and quick, but careful, taking his time at the trick. Hyena is bouncy, foolish, cheerful, and not so much stupid as innocent. The Guinea Hen is also a simple creature, but clearly one that wants to survive. Close the cage door slowly and deliberately so that the action is not lost on the audience. Practice this movement frequently. Rabbit leans the broom against a tree and only picks it up to sprinkle the water. Leave the broom attached to Hyena's paw throughout so that his ineptness is more evident. Practice the movements with the broom and the playing of the sanza frequently. If sprinkling with the broom is too difficult, have Rabbit and Hyena use their paws.

Program Building

Library Programs

Story: A simple African story such as "Why Ostrich Has Such a Long Neck." *Read Aloud:* "Anansi and the Strange Moss Covered Rock." *Music:* Play recorded sanza music as well as other African music as the audience gathers. *Book Talk:* Display and introduce books on African geography, history, and arts. *Short Craft:* Photocopy two or three African mask patterns. The children color and decorate the masks, cut them out, and add a string to hold them in place.

Classroom Study Units

This play is an excellent addition to a unit on Africa. Explore the music and art of Africa. In addition, the theme of small creatures succeeding by using their mental abilities is found in many, many folk tales from all over the world. Introduce as many as you can find. Ask students to rewrite some stories of this type in modern settings.

Bibliography

Picture Books

Anansi and the Strange Moss Covered Rock. Eric Kimmel. Holiday House, 1988. (K–3)

Galimoto. Karen Lynn Williams. Lothrop, 1990. (K–2)

Monkey-Monkey's Trick. Patricia McKissack. Random House, 1988. (1–3)

Rabbit Makes a Monkey of Lion. Verna Aardema. Dial, 1989. (K–1)

Village of Round and Square Houses. Ann Grifalconi. Little, Brown, 1986. (K–3)

Longer Fiction

Ak. Peter Dickinson. Delacorte Press, 1992. (6–8)

Slave Dancer. Paula Fox. Bradbury, 1973. (5–8)

Story Collections

African Folktales. Roger D. Abrahams. Pantheon Books, 1983. (5–adult)

Children of Wax. Alexander McCall Smith. Interlink Books, 1989. (5–8)

The Cow Tail Switch. Harold Courlander. Houghton Mifflin, 1992. (K–6)

The Story Vine. Anne Pellowski. Collier Books, 1984. (K–4)

Tales of an Ashanti Father. Peggy Appiah. Beacon Press, 1967. (K–6)

When Hippo Was Hairy. Nick Greaves. Barrons, 1988. (K–4)

Nonfiction Africa

African Journey. John Haisson. Macmillan, 1987. (5–8)

Ashanti to Zulu: African Traditions. Margaret Musgrove. Dial, 1976. (3–5)

Celebrations of African Heritage. Warren Halliburton. Crestwood House, 1992. (3–6)

Cooking the African Way. Constance Nabwire. The Lerner Group, 1988. (3–6)

Hyena Day. Robert Caputo and Miriam Hsia. Coward McCann, 1978. (1–3)

Hyenas. Alice Hopf. Dodd Mead, 1983. (K–3)

Hyenas. Lynn Stone. Rourke Corporation, 1990. (K–5)

Rabbits and Hares. Colleen Stanley Bare. Dodd Mead, 1983. (4–6)

Media

Chaminuka Dumisani Maraire (compact disc). Dumisani Laraire. Music of the World, 1989.

Discovering the Music of Africa (video recording). Hollywood Select Video, 1987.

Mbira Music Spirit of the People (video recording). Simon Bright. Films for the Humanities, 1993.

Mufaro's Beautiful Daughters (video recording). Reading Rainbow Series. Great Plains National, 1988.

8

Rumplestilsken

Performers: grades 5 through 8
Audience: kindergarten through 3

Cast: Narrator
Father
King
Daughter/Queen
Rumplestilsken
Ralph, a servant
Gillian, a maid

Props: Three piles of straw, small, medium, large; three piles of gold thread small, medium and large; spinning wheel; baby wrapped in a blanket; and book.

Set: A castle.

Narrator: Once upon a time there was a kingdom ruled by a King who was kind and friendly and almost—but not quite—wise. He had one fault, and it was a pretty bad one. He loved gold far too much. He had a lot of gold, so this fault didn't get him into too much trouble. However, the people knew that until he got over this love of gold he would not be a wise man. In this kingdom there lived a man who was very poor. His only treasure was his beautiful daughter, and he believed her to be a trea-

73

sure greater than gold or jewels. The man bragged about his daughter everywhere and told everyone about her great beauty and her skill at spinning, weaving, and all needle arts. And although she was very beautiful and very skillful, her father did not always tell the exact truth. One day he had a chance to speak to the King.

Exit Narrator stage left. Father enters stage right and King enters stage left with Ralph.

Father: Oh! It's the King! *Rushes over to King.* Your Highness, may I speak to you?

King: Of course. Speak up, my good man, speak up.

Father: Uh, I have a daughter who is the most beautiful young woman in the land. She is very clever, too. Why, she can spin wool and linen into thread so fine you can hardly see it.

King: Yes, well, that's very fine. Now good day to you. Come over to visit again sometime. Bring your daughter if you like.

Father: Sir! My daughter can spin straw into gold!

King: What's that! Now that is a skill that interests me. Ralph, go with this man to his house and bring his daughter back to the palace. We must test this skill of hers at once. Quickly, quickly!

Ralph: Yes sir! Right away! *Exits with Father stage right.*

Father: Wait a minute! I didn't mean . . . Oh dear!

Father and Ralph exit stage right. Ralph returns with daughter. Her head is down, hands to face.
Ralph: Your Highness. This is my daughter.

Daughter: Your Highness?

King: Are you the young lady who can spin straw into gold?

Daughter: My father exaggerates a tiny, tiny bit. I can spin wool into the fines of yarn, but I cannot spin straw into gold . . . not for my dear father, and not even for you, Your Highness.

King: What?! I have been deceived? Well, we shall see. Ralph, bring straw! *Ralph bows, exits stage left, and returns with straw, which he places center stage.* Do you see that pile of straw, my dear? You must spin that straw into gold by tomorrow morning or—let me see—what would be a suitable punishment? Aha! You and your father will be put to death. *To audience.* I know that seems harsh, boys and girls, but that is how kings are supposed to behave in stories, and I am a king after all. *King and Ralph exit stage right.*

Daughter: Oh no! What shall I do? I cannot spin straw into gold. Oh Father, you foolish, foolish man. *Sobs.*

Enter Rumplestilsken stage left.

Rumplestilsken: Whatever is all this noise about? Will you please stop that crying young woman? A person cannot hear himself think.

Daughter: Oh! Who are you?

Rumplestilsken: Never mind. What's the trouble here?

Daughter: Well, *sniff.* I must spin all that straw into gold by tomorrow morning or I will die and my father will die, and I don't have the slightest idea how to spin straw into gold. *Sobs.*

Rumplestilsken: Oh, don't start that crying business again. I can spin straw into gold. What will you give me if I do it for you, hmmm?

Daughter: I have a gold ring. It belonged to my mother.

Rumplestilsken: Let's have it. *They touch hands.* Now out of my way so I can work.

He jumps at straw and wrestles it around, then disappears below level of stage and returns with gold. Appropriate sound effects should accompany this.

Rumplestilsken: There you are, Missy. Say hi to the King for me. *Disappears stage left.*

Daughter: Oh my! What a strange creature. He is talented though. I hope the King will be pleased. Oh, here he comes.

King: Enters stage right. Good morning, my dear. Ah! *Sees gold.* Very nice! Very, very nice. Hmmm. I suppose that means you have passed the test. But, it might have been a coincidence. We had better have another test. More straw!

Ralph enters stage right with a larger pile of straw, puts it down center stage, and exits stage right pushing gold ahead of him.

King: Now, my dear, you must spin this straw into gold by morning, or you know what will happen. *Exits stage right.*

Daughter: What a greedy King! And he doesn't keep promises either. I'm so mad I could spit!

Enter Rumplestilsken stage left.

Rumplestilsken: Young ladies do not spit.

Daughter: Oh, it's you.

Rumplestilsken: I would think you would be glad to see me. I did save your life, you know. What's this, more straw?

Daughter: Yes, and I am to spin it into gold or Mister Greedypants King will put me and my dear old daddy to death. Can you help me? Please?

Rumplestilsken: Oh, I suppose I could help. Do you have any more rings?

Daughter: No, but I have a necklace with a moonstone in it. It's only a semi-precious stone, I know, but it is beautifully carved.

Rumplestilsken: Let's see it.*They touch hands.* Hmm. Interesting. Okay. Out of my way. *Business with straw is repeated.*

Rumplestilsken: There you are. Later! *Exits stage left.*

Daughter: Goodness! He moves so quickly. Well this should satisfy that King.

Enter King stage right.

King: Very nice! Even better quality than yesterday. I am almost convinced. I believe that we need one more test. *To audience.* In fairy stories there must be three tests, you know. Yes. One more test. More straw! *Gillian enters stage right and puts down even larger pile of straw at center stage.* What happened to Ralph?

Gillian: He strained his back on the last bundle of gold, so I have to do his work for him, Sir. *Exits stage right pushing gold ahead of her.*

King: Hm. Pity. Well, young lady, there you are. Now, if you spin that straw into gold, your life will be spared and your father's life will be spared. Wait. I have an idea. I just thought of a wonderful reward for you. You will be my wife! You will be Queen. Won't that be nice? Happy spinning, dear. *Exits stage right.*

Daughter: Well, maybe I don't want to be a queen, you old promise breaker, you, you greedy guts you, you . . .

Enter Rumplestilsken stage left.

Rumplestilsken: I see you have more straw. I guess that King doesn't keep promises.

Daughter: Ha! He doesn't know the meaning of the word promise. I must spin this into gold and then marry him and become Queen. Queen! Of all the boring jobs. I wanted to be a forest ranger.

Rumplestilsken: You don't say. Well, what will you give me if I spin this into gold? You don't happen to have a tiara, do you?

Daughter: Of course not. What would a poor man's daughter be doing with a tiara? I don't have anything left. *Sobs.*

Rumplestilsken: I guess you are going to die then. Unless . . . When you are married to the King and you have a little baby prince or princess, you could promise to give that baby to me. If you do that, I'll spin this straw into gold.

Daughter: Give you my baby? Never! *Starts to leave.* Of course, the King probably didn't mean that part about me being Queen. After all, we know that he is not good at keeping promises. Okay, I'll do it.

Rumplestilsken: All right! Here we go. *Does straw and gold business again.* Done! I'll see you when I come to get the baby, dearie! Bye! *Exit Rumplestilsken stage left.*

Daughter: The King should be satisfied with this.

Enter King stage right.

King: Magnificent! You are saved, my dear. And your father is saved too. And, you will be my Queen. *Reaches out to hug her.*

Daughter: Backs away. Oh, that isn't necessary. I'll just go home to my father. I am quite content.

King: Nonsense, my dear. I have grown quite fond of you. You are very beautiful, as your father said. You were very understanding about those tests with the straw. I am terribly sorry. The sight of all that gold must have affected my brain. My friend King Midas had the same problem. I will appoint a royal treasurer to look after the gold, and I will never test you again.

Daughter: Well, since you are sorry. *To audience.* And he is quite good-looking for a King.

King: I am truly, truly sorry. And very ashamed of my greed. Forgive me, my lady. From this moment I will be free of the love for gold, and I will never break a promise to you again.

Daughter: Then I will be your wife, if I can be a forest ranger as well.

King: Of course! Splendid! Now let's go tell your father and make plans for a happy wedding with lots of games, and a great chocolate cake, and music, and dancing!

King and Daughter exit stage right. A sign reading "Time Passes" moves from stage left to stage right. Daughter enters stage right, wearing a robe and forest ranger's hat with a crown for a hatband. She is carrying a baby in her arms and singing "Hush Little Baby." Enter Rumplestilsken stage left.

Rumplestilsken: I've come for the child, Queenie. Give it here!

Daughter: Ohhh! No! No! Go away, you dreadful creature. Go away! You will never take my baby!

Rumplestilsken: Dreadful creature? Ungrateful girl. Remember when I spun that straw into gold for you. You didn't call me names and send me away then. You promised me that baby, and you must give it to me. Hand over that brat right now!

Daughter: Never! Never! I will not. I cannot. Please. You may have all my jewels, even my crown—anything but my child.

Rumplestilsken: No. I want that baby. There is only one way that I will release you from your promise. You must guess my name. I will return three times. You will have three guesses each time I return. If you do not guess my name by the third visit, the baby is mine! *Exits stage left.)*

Daughter: Oh dear! Gillian!

Gillian: Enters stage right. Yes, Your Highness.

Daughter: Gillian dear, please take the baby and put her in the royal nursery. Lock the door and do not open it for anyone except me or the King.

Gillian: Yes, Your Highness. *Bows and exits with baby.*

Daughter: Oh my! How will I find out what his name is? Maybe it is in a library book. *Reaches below and gets a book. Looks in it.* Let's see. Hmm! *Sigh.*

Enter Rumplestilsken stage left.

Rumplestilsken: I'm back, dearie. What's my name?

Daughter: Is it Old King Cole?

Rumplestilsken: No!

Daughter: Is it Tom Thumb?

Rumplestilsken: No!

Daughter: Is it Jack the Giant Killer?

Rumplestilsken: No! Ha, ha, ha! *Exits stage left.*

Daughter: Well, I guess that was not the right book. *Tosses it behind her.* Oh no! Here he comes again.

Enter Rumplestilsken stage left.

Rumplestilsken: So, fine lady, what is my name?

Daughter: Is it . . . *name of child in audience?*

Rumplestilsken: No!

Daughter: Is it . . . *name of another child in audience?*

Rumplestilsken: No!

Daughter: Is it . . . *name of third child in audience?*

Rumplestilsken: No, no, no. I will be back one more time. Only three more guesses. Soon the baby will be mine! Have its suitcase packed and ready. Ha, ha, ha! *Exits stage left.*

Daughter: Oh, oh, what shall I do? I need help. *Rushes from one side of the stage to the other, stops and looks at audience.* Boys and girls, will you help me please? I must know the creature's name. Can you tell me? Do you know what the creature's name is? What? Rumplestilsken? What an odd name. Are you sure? Well, all right. I will try it. I hope that you are right. Oh, oh, here he comes again.

Enter Rumplestilsken stage left.

Rumplestilsken: Hi, ho, lady. What is your name? No, no, that isn't right. What is my name?

Daughter: Ah, creature, could your name be . . . *name of child in audience*?

Rumplestilsken: No! That's one.

Daughter: Could your name be . . . *name of another child in audience*?

Rumplestilsken: No, no! That's two. Come on, Queenie, what's guess number three?

Daughter: Could it be that your name is Rumplestilsken?!

Rumplestilsken: What, what, what, what?! Who told you? Who told you? Was it you, you naughty, wicked girls and boys. AIEEEEE! *Rushes around stage.* Pip, pip, pip! *Disappears.*

Daughter: Very good! That is the end of him! Thank you, my friends. You saved my baby. Would you like to know the end of the story? This is what happens. Rumplestilsken never ever came back and was never even heard of again. The King grew nicer and more wise and generous all his long life. We had two more children—twins. The trees in the royal forest grew tall and healthy, and we lived happily ever after. The end. The end. The end!

Playing Notes

Puppeteers and Puppets

Classroom or Workshop Production

Involve more children in this play by adding a donkey that accompanies the Father and a snooty dog that accompanies the King. Add a wedding scene in which a clergy person puppet and many puppets sing "Here Comes the Bride," "Joy to the World" by Three Dog Night, "Going to the Chapel," "I'm Getting Married in the Morning," or some other appropriate song.

Library Production

If you eliminate the servants, this play can be performed by two puppeteers. One puppeteer is the King and the Father. The other is the Daughter and Rumplestilsken. The King puppeteer must manipulate the straw and gold. Rumplestilsken makes the spinning sounds. The Queen takes the baby offstage and comes back with the library book.

Props and Scenery

The scene is a palace. Decorate the front of the stage with construction paper cutouts of stone walls, moats, formal gardens, and ladies and gentlemen in fancy dress doing fancy stuff. Use velvet draperies and golden cords to decorate the playing area. Glue straw or narrow strips of yellow construction paper onto paper cups to make piles of straw. Glue gold tinsel to paper cups to make piles of gold. Attach small dowels or straws to the inside of the cups for the prop handler to move them around. Use sturdy paper cups or they will collapse under the glue. Strong cardboard tubes also would work well. Make small, medium, and large piles of straw and gold. The library book is a rectangle of white paper inside a rectangle of colored paper, folded in half and stapled. Make a spinning wheel of construction paper or felt cut out and glued to cardboard. The spinning wheel is on far stage left on the edge of the stage. Rumplestilsken moves the straw to the spinning wheel and places the gold at center stage. Mime the action of handing over the ring and the necklace; these props are too small to handle. The baby is a cylindrical shape wrapped securely in a blanket so that it can be passed from Queen to Gillian.

Action

The Father bobs and bows a lot. The King is ponderous and wears lots of gold. The scenes between the Daughter and Rumplestilsken are lively. Rumplestilsken moves quickly, but stops when speaking. He speaks in a staccato rhythm, but not so quickly that he is not understood. He whirls and swoops about when he enters and exits. When he exits at the end, he should hop and sputter, faster and higher, before he finally swoops quickly off to the side. Use a slide whistle to punctuate his actions. The daughter is emotional but determined. As Queen she is strong and confident and very much a mother.

Program Building

Library Programs

Stories: Tell the story of King Midas. *Read Aloud:* "The Emperor and the Kite." *Short Craft:* Make necklaces from macaroni that has been painted gold

Longer Programs and Classroom Units

Enliven a study of gold and other minerals with a production of *Rumplestilsken.* Collect and display maps of places where gold has been important in the history of the area: California, Alaska, South Africa, for example. Display a chart of the elements and discuss the properties of gold. Compare it with other metals. Make a list of the folk tales and fairy tales in which gold plays a significant part. Ask students to create and display illustration for these stories. Make available books about gold jewelry in museum collections. Study the lives of some important queens in history.

Bibliography

Picture Books

Emperor and the Kite. Jane Yolen. Philomel, 1988. (K–3)

Golden Goose. Susan Saunders. Scholastic, 1988. (K–3)

King Midas and the Golden Touch. Harcourt Brace Jovanovich, 1987. (K–3)

Longer Fiction

Bite of the Gold Bug. Barthe DeClements. Viking, 1992. (2–4)

By the Great Horn Spoon. Sid Fleischmann. Little, Brown, 1963. (4–6)

Chang's Paper Pony. Eleanor Coerr. Harper and Row, 1988. (2–4)

A Golden Touch. Annabel Johnson. Harper and Row, 1963. (3–5)

Trap of Gold. Alison Smith. Dodd Mead, 1985. (4–6)

Nonfiction

The Alaska Gold Rush. May McNeer. Random House, 1962. *(4–6)*

Gold and Other Precious Metals. Charles Coombs. Morrow, 1981. *(3–5)*

Gold of Greece. Mousein Benake. Dallas Museum of Art, 1990. (Adult)

Gold: The Fascinating Story of the Noble Metal Through the Ages. David Cohn. Lippincott, 1976. (4–6)

Gold: The True Story of Why People Search for It, Mine It, Trade It, Steal It, Mint It, Hoard It, Shape It, Wear It, Fight and Kill for It. Milton Meltzer. Harper Collins, 1993. (4–8)

The Great American Gold Rush. Rhoda Blumberg. Bradbury Press, 1989. (4–8)

The Story of the Gold at Sutter's Mill. R. Conrad Stein. Children's Press, 1981.

The Treasures of Tutankhamen. British Museum. Viking Press, 1973. (Adult)

Biographies

Henry VIII. Dorothy Turner. Bookwright, 1987. *(5–7)*

Queen Eleanor, Independent Spirit of the Medieval World. Polly Brooks. Harper, 1986. (6–8)

Queen Elizabeth I. Dorothy Turner. Watts, 1987. (5–7)

Shaka: King of the Zulus. Diane Stanley and Peter Vennema. Morrow, 1988. (2–4)

Music

"Chapel of Love." *Experience the Divine: Greatest Hits.* Bette Midler. Atlantic, 1993.

"I'm Getting Married in the Morning." *My Fair Lady.* Columbia Records, 1976.

"Joy to the World." *The Big Chill* (soundtrack). Motown, 1984.

9

Sleeping Beauty

Performers: grades 4 through 8
Audience: grades kindergarten through 3

Cast: Dragon Olivetti (Narrator)
Queen
King Albertus
Giles
Aunt Awgusta
Aunt Clara
Princess Rosamunde
Prince

Props: Paper airplane, scroll of presents, spinning wheel, wall of thorns, time tree, numbers for the time tree.

Set: Castle with a rose hedge on stage right, time tree on stage left.

Enter Dragon stage left.

Dragon: Hello, boys and girls. I'm Olivetti Dragon and I am going to tell you about our play. It's called *Sleeping Beauty*. Now maybe you know that once upon a time there was a King and a Queen who were very sad. I mean saaaad! They were sad

83

because they had no children. No children! Not one. Then, joy of all joys, treasure of all treasures, that Queen had a beautiful baby girl. A daughter! The Queen and the King named her Rosamunde and they planned to have a big party to celebrate her birth. Now Rosamunde had thirteen aunts. Imagine! Thirteen aunts! They were good aunts, except for one who had a bad temper. Of course, they all wanted to come to the party for Rosamunde. Oh, here comes the King. The play has begun.

Exit Dragon stage left. Enter King stage right.

King: Okay, Giles. Let her rip!

Giles: Offstage. Yes Your Majesty! *A paper airplane flies from behind the stage and into the audience.*

King: Fantastic! It went over the moat and into the enchanted forest! Let's make another one.

King turns and starts to go off stage right. Queen enters stage left.

Queen: Oh dear! Oh dear! Albertus! Stop playing that silly game and help me. We have a terrible problem. We do not have enough chairs or crystal goblets or golden plates to have all the aunts at the party. Someone will have to be left out.

King: Returns to Queen at center stage. Why don't we have paper plates and cups? I saw some neat ones with black and white cows on them.

Queen: Don't be ridiculous, dear.

King: I'm sorry.

Queen: Quite. You see, the only way we will have enough chairs and china is if we do not invite one of the aunts. We must decide which one to leave out.

King: Well, I suggest leaving out Awful Awgusta. She's very crabby and has no sense of humor.

Queen: Awgusta is not awful, just a bit difficult. However, I think you are right. Perhaps she will not notice. She's very busy making sour pickles just now.

King: Let's send out the royal invitations then. I'm going to play with the baby. *Exit King stage right.*

Queen: Giles!

Giles: Enters stage left and bows. Yes, Your Majesty.

Queen: There is a box of invitations by the front door. Please deliver them to the aunts. But—and this is very important—do not leave one at Awgusta's. Do not even go near her house.

Giles: Yes, Your Highness. *Exits stage left.*

Queen: Now, what shall we eat at the party? Hmmm! *Paces back and forth.* We will start with iced zucchini soup. The royal garden is full of zucchini. In fact, if any of you out there would like a zucchini, please help yourself from the basket. We'll have corn muffins with the soup. Then we'll have asparagus crepes and sliced tomatoes and some mushrooms flambe. Albertus loves things that are served on fire. There will be raspberry punch and lemonade to drink. For dessert we will have little meringue swans swimming in chocolate pools.

Enter Giles stage right carrying a large scroll.

Giles: Your Highness, the royal invitations have been delivered. This is a list of the gifts the aunts sent Princess Rosamunde. You and the King are to read the list now.

Queen: Now? Goody. I love presents. And so does the King. *Calls.* Oh King dear.

Enter King stage left.

King: You called, my little rutabaga?

Queen: Yes, pumpkinbread. The aunts have sent tons of presents to Rosamunde, and we are to read the list now.

King: Neat! I love presents! On with it!

Queen: Me first.

Queen takes scroll from Giles and places it on the edge of the stage. One end rolls forward and down the front of the stage. Giles bows and exits stage left behind the King.

Queen: For Rosamunde. A loving heart. Yes. An essential quality, most important for a Princess, or anyone else.

King: For Rosamunde. Wisdom. That's useful.

Queen: For Rosamunde. Beauty. Beauty is handy. No doubt about it.

King: For Rosamunde. A great curve ball. How odd. Wouldn't mind that myself.

85

Queen: For Rosamunde. A love of leafy green vegetables. Very thoughtful.

King: For Rosamunde. The ability to find a rhyme for any word, even orange and silver. Good, good.

Queen: For Rosamunde. A library card. Splendid! Practical and inspirational.

King: For Rosamunde. A lifetime supply of crayons and marker pens in sixty-five colors including fluorescent colors, glitter crayons, and pastels. Wow! I hope she lets me play with them.

Queen: For Rosamunde. A lifetime supply of paper, glue, scissors, and glitter. What fun we will have!

King: For Rosamunde. The ability to solve riddles, puzzles, and secret codes. Neat!

Queen: For Rosamunde. The ability to learn stories and memorize poems. Good. She can tell us stories and recite poems when we cannot fall asleep.

Awgusta: Offstage. Ingrates! Fools! Idiots! Dolts! *Enters stage right.* How dare you fail to invite me to your party for my infant niece. You will regret this. Ohhh, how you will regret this.

King: Now Awgusta, I am sure that when you hear our explanations you will understand.

Awgusta: Twit!

Queen: Awgusta dear, please listen.

Awgusta: Bubble-head! I will not listen. I will not understand. I will not forgive. Did you think I would overlook this insult?

Queen: Well, we hoped you would not notice, being so busy with the pickles and all.

King: Besides, you know how you hate crowds.

Awgusta: Silence! In spite of your bad manners and stupidity, I will give the Princess a present. She will grow and thrive until she is fifteen years old. Then she will prick her finger on a spinning wheel and die! Ha, ha, ha, hee, hee, hee. *Exits stage right in a sweeping rush, laughing madly.*

Queen: Ohh! Boo hoo, boo hoo, boo hoo.

King: Oh my dear, what shall we do? *Hugs Queen.* Whatever shall we do. *Sobs. Enter thirteenth aunt, Clara, stage left.*

Clara: I saw Awgusta rushing out of here. What has she been up to? Oh, my goodness, what is wrong my sister, my brother?

Queen: Sobbing. Oh, Clara, because we did not invite her to our baby's party, Awgusta has placed a curse on little Princess Rosamunde. She is to prick her finger on a spinning wheel when she is fifteen years old and then she will die. *More sobbing.*

Clara: That is horrible. I did not think that even Awgusta would do anything so terrible. Calm yourselves, dears. I must think what to do. *Hands to head.* I have an idea!

King: Yes?

Queen: What is it, Clara?

Clara: Well, I have not given Rosamunde a gift yet. I was going to give her a green thumb, but never mind. I cannot remove Awgusta's curse, but I can weaken it considerably. I will give the Princess Rosamunde this gift: When she is fifteen, she will indeed prick her finger on a spinning wheel, but she will not die. She will fall asleep for seven years. The whole kingdom will fall asleep with her—all the people. All the beasts. After seven years of sleeping, a prince with a pure heart will come to the kingdom. He will kiss the sleeping Princess, and that kiss will awaken her. All the kingdom will awaken, the curse will be broken, and happiness will return to the kingdom.

Queen: Dear Clara, thank you, sister. *They hug.*

King: Thank you, Clara. But I am going to have every spinning wheel in the kingdom destroyed. The Princess will never set eyes upon a spinning wheel.

All exit stage left comforting one another. Enter Olivetti stage left, crying and sniffing.

Olivetti: Oh boys and girls. This is so sad. *Sniff.* The Princess grew up into a dear sweet person with a loving heart, wisdom, and a great curve ball, and all those other nifty gifts. The king did have every spinning wheel in the kingdom destroyed, and the Princess did not even know what a spinning wheel was. Perhaps you don't either. It looks like this. *Reaches below stage level and brings up spinning wheel, then puts it on center stage.* People used them to spin the wool from sheep into yarn. Fifteen years passed.

This card is removed from the time tree. Exit Olivetti stage left. Enter Awgusta stage right.

Awgusta: Ha! There is my spinning wheel. *Sits at wheel.* I will show that King and Queen. Not invite me, Awgusta the Difficult, to a party? Well, they'll be sorry. I know this seems harsh, boys and girls, but that's the way the story goes, and somebody has to be the bad guy. *Sings to the tune "East Side West Side" or any tune.* "Spinning, spinning, spinning is a joy."

Enter Princess stage left.

Princess: Oh! Hello, Aunt Awgusta. What is that?

Awgusta: Hi, dearie. This is a spinning wheel. It spins wool into yarn. Like this: *Sings.* "Spinning, spinning, spinning is a joy."

Princess: Do you suppose that I might try spinning?

Awgusta: Certainly, my pet. Put your hand right here.

Princess: Okay. Oh! Ouch! I pricked my finger. *Slumps onto stage left, asleep.*

Awgusta: Ha, ha! I am avenged.

Awgusta swoops out, stage right, taking spinning wheel. Enter Olivetti stage left, behind and past sleeping Princess.

Olivetti: Aunt Awgusta's curse, with Clara's changes, fell over the kingdom. The Princess is asleep. The King and Queen are also asleep. All the aunts are asleep except for Awgusta, who moved to Antarctica. The rest of the kingdom, including the animals, birds, fish, and spiders, fell asleep and they all snore. *Sound of snoring from backstage.* I'm feeling a little sleepy myself. *Yawns.* Seven years passed while they slept.

Numbers 3, 2, and 1 are removed from the tree. Dragon snores and slips down behind stage. Lots of snoring as the wall of thorns is added to the rose hedge. Enter Prince stage right and stops at wall of thorns.

Prince: What a dense rose hedge. *Snore.* What is that sound? It sounds like snoring. *Snore.* Hmm? I wonder if this could be the castle where the enchanted Princess Rosamunde lies asleep. She must sleep until a prince with a pure heart kisses her. Do you suppose that I might have a pure heart? Lots of princes have tried to get through this dense and thorny hedge, but none could because they did not have a pure hearts, whatever one is. Oh my. What a lovely rose! *Touches rose and the hedge sinks away.* Wow. Maybe I really do have a pure heart. Now, I wonder where that Princess is. *Notices Rosamunde.* This must Rosamunde. She's wearing a crown. Hmm. How beautiful she is! A little dusty though. Well, if I am a prince with a pure heart, I can break the spell with a kiss. We will see. *Kisses her and jumps back quickly.*

Princess: Oh. What was that? Who are you?

Prince: I am a prince with a pure heart. You have been under a spell. You have been asleep for seven years. The whole kingdom and every living thing in it have been asleep. When I kissed you, you woke up.

Princess: Where are my mother the Queen and my father the King?

Prince: They are asleep. I can see them in the courtyard along with all the lords and ladies and cows and dogs and cats and everybody.

Princess: I am going to wake them up and tell them that the spell is over. And I will introduce you to them.

Exit Princess and Prince stage right. Enter Olivetti stage left.

Olivetti: Oh my, ahhhh! Excuse my yawning. Well, Princess Rosamunde and the Prince with a pure heart fell in love—of course. Then they were married. They sent a wedding invitation to Awgusta in Antarctica because they didn't want to annoy her, but she said she was too busy to attend anyway. And so they all lived happily ever after. The end.

Playing Notes

Puppeteers and Puppets

Classroom Production

There are eight puppeteers in the play as it is written. You will also need two prop handlers. Involve more children by including the other eleven aunts. The aunts can be animal puppets in wigs and hats if you don't have enough human puppets. The aunts bring their gifts to the King and Queen one at a time and each aunt announces what the gift is. The King and Queen, Rosamunde, and the Prince should be human puppets. If you do not have a dragon puppet, turn Olivetti's role into any puppet you have. To include even more children, introduce a puppet chorus to sing a lullaby during the seven-year sleep period. This chorus can be the aunts in white collars. Use a puppet conductor who makes extravagant gestures.

Library Production

Sleeping Beauty can be performed with two puppeteers if you leave out Giles and the time tree. One puppeteer is the King, Awgusta, and the Prince. The other puppeteer is Olivetti, the Queen, Rosamunde, and Clara. If the changes for Olivetti are too difficult, this part can be given to Clara or to a human narrator who steps in front of the stage to introduce the play. Giles is a voice offstage for the business with the paper airplane. The King delivers the invitations and brings the scroll with the list of presents back onstage. Eliminate the time tree and mark the passage of time with a sign raised and lowered from behind the stage. Enlist a third person as helper if you can.

Scenery and Props

The passage of time is an important element in this story. The time tree is an effective visual aid in counting the years of Rosamunde's growth to age fifteen, and the seven years of her cursed sleep. Write numbers on Post-its and attach them to the tree. A servant puppet lifts them from the tree, or they might be pushed off with a stick. The tree itself is a cardboard cutout dec-

orated with paint or felt. It would be quite tedious to sit through the removal of fifteen cards, so have number combinations on the tree—three fives for fifteen, and a three and four for seven.

The rose hedge is simply cardboard painted to look like a hedge and mounted on rods. Brightly colored felt glued to cardboard is also effective. Four or five sections mounted one behind the other and slightly staggered will give the impression of density. Some large, sharp thorns sticking out from the edges are effective. Move the hedge up from below the stage level and place it behind the rose bush. This coincides with the action of the time cards flying off of the tree during Rosamunde's sleep. It sinks slowly away when the Prince touches the rose.

The spinning wheel is painted on cardboard, cut out, and mounted on a rod. Again, cutout felt glued to card stock is effective. The scroll is a two-inch by five-inch piece of cream-colored felt that is rolled up. Glue a small stick across the front edge so that it will fall over the front of the stage as the King and Queen read from the middle section.

Action

Aunt Awgusta's comings and goings are swift and accompanied by a slide whistle or siren whistle. Accompany the Prince's discovery that he has a pure heart with a bird song whistle. Everyone backstage should snore. Practice different kinds of snoring, whistling snores, short barking snores, honking snores, snores punctuated by lip smacking, sighing, groaning, and muttering. Use all of these snores during the long sleep scene, as long as the audience is amused. Agree on a signal to stop the snoring when the Prince moves onstage.

Program Building

Library Programs

Stories: "Rip Van Winkle" or "The Boy of the Three Year Nap." *Read Aloud: The Napping House.* Songs: "Ten in a Bed," or a lullaby. *Short Craft:* Each child makes a sign to hang on their bedroom door. The word "Awake" is on one side, "Asleep" on the other. Prepare the signs ahead of time so the children can decorate them and add the cord to hang them.

Longer Programs and Classroom Study Units

Introduce a unit on sleep. Discuss true hibernation and the long deep sleep of wintering animals. Make a mural of sleeping animals in several different environments. Study human sleep and how our brains and muscles behave in sleep. Make a mural or models of the sleeping people and animals in the kingdom of Sleeping Beauty. Collect lullabies from many cultures. Make lists of birthday presents like the ones given to Rosamunde to give to a newborn.

Bibliography

Picture Books

Abiyoyo. Pete Seeger. Simon and Schuster, 1994. (P–K)

Dreams. Ezra Jack Keats. Macmillan, 1974. (P–K)

Ira Sleeps Over. Bernard Waber. Houghton Mifflin, 1972. (K–2)

May We Sleep Here Tonight? Tan Koide. Athenaeum, 1983. (P–K)

The Napping House. Audrey Wood. Harcourt Brace Jovanovich, 1984. (P–K)

Ten in a Bed. Mary Reed. Joy Street Books, 1988. (P–K)

Longer Fiction

And God Bless Me: Prayers, Lullabies and Dream Poems. Lee Bennett Hopkins. Random House, 1982. (P–3)

Boy of the Three Year Nap. Dianne Snyder. Houghton Mifflin, 1988. (K–2)

Go Tell Aunt Rhody. Macmillan, 1986. (P–K)

Hush Little Baby. Pantheon; 1984. (P–K)

Lullabies and Night Songs. William Engvick. Harper and Row, 1965. (P–2)

The Lullaby Songbook. Jane Yolen. Harcourt Brace Jovanovich, 1986. (P–J)

Medieval Feast. Aliki. Harper amd Row, 1983. (2–6)

Rip Van Winkle. Thomas Locker, adapter. Dial, 1988. (3–4)

Tournament of Knights. Joe Lasker. Harper and Row. 1986. (3–6)

Music

Lullabies and Laughter. Pat Carfa. LL records, 1983. (P–1)

Lullaby Magic I and II. Joanie Bartels. Discovery Music, 1985 and 1987. (P–K)

Nonfiction

Animals in Winter. Susana Riha. Carolrhoda, 1989. (3–4)

Sleep and Dreams. Alvin and Virginia Silverstein. Lippincott, 1974. (6–8)

Sleep: Do Not Disturb: Mysteries of Animal Hibernation and Sleep. Margery Facklam. Little, Brown, 1989. (3–5)

Sleeping and Dreaming. Rita Milios. Children's Press, 1987. (2–4)

Sleeping Beauty: The Story of the Ballet. Linda Jennings. Hodder and Stoughton, 1987. (K–3)

Ways Animals Sleep. Jane R. McCauley. National Geographic, 1983. (P–3)

Weaving. Susie O'Reilly. Thomason Learning, 1993. (4–8)

Why Do We Need Sleep. Isaac Asimov and Carrie Dierks. Stevens, 1993. (4–6)

10

The Three Little Pigs

Performers: grades 4 through 6
Audience: preschool through grade 3

Cast: Mother Pig, dressed in fancy traveling hat
Pig 1, wears glasses
Pig 2, wears bow tie
Pig 3, wears hair ribbon
Man who sells straw
Man who sells sticks
Wolf

Props: House of straw; house of sticks; house of bricks; bundles of straw, sticks, and bricks; Girl Scout disguise; mock *National Geographic* magazine.

Set: Trees on both sides of stage to suggest country setting.

Mother Pig enters stage right, moves to center stage.

Mother Pig: Children, children. Come here, darlings.

Pig 1 enters stage right.

Pig 1: Yes, Mom.

Pig 3 enters stage left.

Pig 3: Here we are, Mommy.
Pig 2 enters stage left.

Pig 2: We were playing Nintendo.

Mother Pig: Yes, well, exactly. Life isn't all Nintendo and balloons, you know. I have decided to retire from the mothering business. So, you piglets are on your own. Here is $1.98 for each of you and some coupons. Let me know when you have made your fortunes, and I'll come for a visit. Goodbye. I'm off to Hawaii. Aloha, aloha, darlings. Aloha. *exit stage right rear*

Pig 1: What? Well, hmm.

Pig 2: Bye, Mom! Well, what's next?

Pig 1: Guess it's time to go seek my fortune.

Pig 2: Me too, I'm going to seek my fortune too. *Exits stage left.*

Pig 3: I think I will begin my search at the library. I am going to look up books on housing materials, career opportunities, and things like that. *Exits stage left.*

Pig 1: Gee, $1.98 is not very much money. What can I buy for $1.98?

Straw Man: Enters stage left. Straw! Straw for sale. Nice, dry, scratchy straw. Only $1.98 a bundle!

Pig 1: Mr. Straw Man, could a person or a pig make a house with that stuff?

Straw Man: Sure! It would be light and airy, and if you got hungry you could chew on it a bit. It would make a great house.

Pig 1: Well, I'll take a bundle then. Here's $1.98.

Straw Man: Thanks, Pig. Good luck! *Exits stage left.*

Pig 1: Let's see, it can't be that hard to make a house. I'll just put the straw down here and get to work.

Pig 1 works just below the edge of the stage. The tips of his ears show now and then. Grunts, panting, banging, sawing, and drilling noises are heard. Straw flies up in the air now and then. At last a clumsy straw house rises up from behind the stage.

Pig 1: What a glorious edifice! Whew! I'm exhausted! I'm going to go inside and have a little nap. *Goes into house; sound of snoring comes from house.*

Wolf enters stage left singing "Over the River and Through the Woods." He stops when he sees house.

Wolf: Will you look at that? A straw house. *Looks in window.* There's a pig in there! *Snore from house.* It's asleep. Heh, heh, heh. *Tries window.* Window's too small. *Tries door.* Door's locked. Let's try a trick. Pigs are not very smart. *Knocks on door.* Piggy, oh little piggy. *Sweetly.* Let me come in.

Pig 1: What? Who's out there? *Looks out window.* Oh no! It's the Big Bad Wolf. You want me to let you come in? Don't be silly, wolfie. I'm not going to let you in, not by the hair on my chinny chin chin.

Wolf: Come on piggy, let me in.

Pig 1: No! Go away!

Wolf: Well then, I'll huff and I'll puff and I'll blow your house down. Here goes. *Blows lightly, but house stands.* Hm, this house is sturdier than it looks. Boys and girls out there, would you help me blow this house down. You will? Great! On the count of three then. One, two, three! *Blows and house falls down.*

Pig 1: Help, help!

Pig runs away stage left, changes direction, and exits stage right. Wolf wheels around confused.

Wolf: Where is that pig? Is it out there, boys and girls? No? Oh no! I'll have to eat at McDonald's again.

Wolf exits stage right. Enter man with bundles of sticks stage right.

Stick Man: Sticks, sticks for sale. A million uses, all sizes. Sticks for sale. Only $1.98!

Pig 2: Enters stage left. Hello, Stick Man. Say, could you build a house with those sticks?

Stick Man: Sure could! Easy as pie! Stick houses practically build themselves. And nothing can match a stick house for rustic charm.

Pig 2: Sold! Here's your $1.98. *Man gives Pig 2 bundle and exits stage right.* Let's see. I think I'll try a Dutch Colonial design.

Pig 2 works just below edge of stage, tips of ears showing, sticks flying, sound of grunts, pants, hammering, sawing, drilling, etc. Stick house rises up into view.

Pig 2: Fantastic. Even if I do say so myself.

Wolf sings "Whistle While You Work" offstage.

Pig 2: Uh, oh, it's the Big Bad Wolf. I finished my house just in time. Good thing I put a good strong lock on the door. *Goes into house.*

Wolf: Enters stage left whistling. What's this? Another silly-looking house. You know, this might just be another little piggy's house. *Creeps up and looks in window.* It is! It is a little piggy's house. Ah, little pig, oh, little pig. *Sweetly.* Let me come in.

Pig 2: You must think I'm a silly pig, Big Bad Wolf. Well, I'm not, and you are not coming in. Not by the hair of my chinny chin chin.

Wolf: Oh dear. Boy and girls, we are going to have to do that huffing and puffing stuff again. Will you help me blow this house down? Okay? On the count of three. One, two, three—blow! *House does not fall down.* I guess this house is stronger than it looks. Let's try again, and this time you adults out there. You blow too. Ready? One, two, three—blow! *House falls down.*

Pig 2: Help, help! The Big Bad Wolf is after me! Help, help! *Chase scene as before, and Pig 2 disappears.*

Wolf: Hey, where is that piggy? Where is it? These fat little piggies are faster than they look. And I missed my chance at another pig dinner. *Whiny.* It's McDonald's again for me.

Wolf exits stage right. Pig 3 enters stage left with a load of bricks.

Pig 3: Whew. These bricks are very heavy. But the library book on construction did say that bricks were the strongest building material one could use. And the bricks cost $1.98, just like the straw and sticks my brothers used. I wonder how they are doing. You know, I really think you cannot build a strong and sturdy house out of just straw or sticks. Oh well, if their houses do not work out they can come and live with me, and I can beat them at Scrabble every night. Let's see. I believe I will build my house right here, with some windows facing east for the morning sun, and I will put a garden over there.

Pig 3 puts bricks below stage level and begins working. She sings "The Eency Weency Spider." There are sounds of tapping. Pig 3 pushes finished house up to stage level.

Pig 3: There we are. Now that is a house. Strong and sturdy and beautiful. I am feeling a little hungry now with all that work. I think I'll just go inside and make some vegetable soup, and a carrot salad, and maybe an apple pudding for dessert.

Pig 3 enters house and can be seen puttering. Wolf enters stage left.

Wolf: I must be getting old. I just can't seem to catch piggies like I used to. Maybe it's my diet. Not enough leafy green vegetables or something. Hey, look at this. This might be another pig house. I don't know; it's a pretty sturdy-looking house. *Peers in window.* It is a pig house. Must be a smart piggy to have built such a fine house. I'm going to have to use trickery and guile this time. We wolves are very good at trickery and guile. Excuse me a minute. I'm going to get my disguise on. *Exits stage left, puts a green ribbon on head, returns, and knocks.* Oh little pig, little pig, I'm a Girl Scout selling cookies. Please let me come in. *In a high-pitched voice.*

Pig 3: You are not a Girl Scout and, anyway I do not eat cookies. They are bad for your teeth. You are the Big Bad Wolf, and I am not letting you in. Not by the hair of my chinny chin chin.

Wolf: What a smart piggy! I'll try something else. *Exits stage left and returns with* National Geographic *in mouth, then drops it to speak.* Oh little pig, little pig, let me come in. I'm selling subscriptions to the *National Geographic* magazine.

Pig 3: I already have a subscription to the *National Geographic* and you are the Big Bad Wolf. Wolfie, I am not letting you in. Not by the hair of my chinny chin chin.

Wolf: In deep and gruff voice. Then I will huff and I'll puff and I'll blow your house down.

Pig 3: Go right ahead and try, Wolfie. This house is strong and sturdy.

Wolf: Okay, boys and girls. As you have heard, this is a very strong and sturdy house. I'm going to need all of your help. You grown-ups, you teachers and librarians, and moms and dads and grandmas and grandpas, even the babies—you all must help. Let's warm up a little bit. *Short breaths.* Whew, whew, whew, whew. Good. Now we're ready. On the count of three. One, two, three—blow. *Everyone blows. Wolf pants as he talks.* Okay. Now we're really ready. Again. One two three—blow. *Everyone blows. Wolf collapse over edge of stage, panting.* One last try then. Everybody, One, two, three—blow! *Wolf falls backwards and disappears below stage level. He reappears using his mouth and/or paws to pull himself up to stage level, still panting.* Okay. Now I'm really mad. This pig is just too smart. Well, I'll show her. I'm going to go up on the roof and down the chimney into the house. What do you think? Good idea! Cool, huh? What's that? A pot of boiling water? No, a piggy wouldn't do that. Oh well, I am going to try it anyway. *Climbs up roof with great difficulty, slides off, slowly at first and then fast, then lands on ground crying.* Oh, oh, noooo. Ow boo hoo, hoo. Boo, hoo hoo!

Pig 3: Comes out of house. Wolfie, I tried to warn you but you would not listen. Now look at you! You are a mess. Are you through trying to catch piggies?

Wolf: Yes. *Sobs.*

Pig 3: Do you promise that you will never try to catch piggies again?

Wolf: Never, never! I promise, I really, really do!

Pig 3: Good. Now get out of here. I never want to see you around here again! Get out! Shoo! Scoot! Scram!

Pig 3 makes shooing motions and Wolf, whimpering, exits stage left. Pig 1 and Pig 2 enter stage left.

Pig 1: Way to go, Sis. You sure got rid of the Wolf.

Pig 2: And you built a swell house too!

Pig 3: It is quite splendid, isn't it? Would you like to live here with me?

Pigs 1 and 2: Yes! Sure!

Pig 2: And we'll do our own dishes and laundry.

Pig 1: I'll take out the garbage.

Pig 3: Fine! Now let's go in and have some lunch, and then we will play a game of Scrabble. *Exit Pigs 1 and 2 behind house.* Oh, this play is over. The end, the end, the end.

Playing Notes

Puppeteers and Puppets

Classroom Production

There is one puppeteer for each character. Many more children can be involved because of the number of props and the need for sound effects. Sound effects are fun and impressive in this play, and children can use slide whistles, hammers, etc. to make the sounds. Appoint one or two children to be sound technicians and prop managers. Assign them the task of discovering what implements or materials make which sounds. There is quite a bit of interaction between the puppet characters and the audience in this play. Instruct the children who are not in the play to lead the audience in the appropriate responses.

Library Production

Two puppeteers and a helper can perform this play. The Stick Man and the Straw Man become offstage voices. The Pigs must face offstage to talk with them. One puppeteer is Mother Pig, Pig 1, and the Wolf. The other puppeteer is the voices of Stick Man, Straw Man, as well as Pig 2 and Pig 3. The helper manipulates the props. There is a shorter version of this play in the appendix.

If you only have enough puppets for Mother Pig and one piglet, make simple costume changes to identify the different piglets. Eliminate the scenes where all three piglets appear together. For example, Pig 1 appears with Mother Pig alone and agrees to pass the message about the mother's plan on to the others. In the last scene, Pig 3 exits to find her brothers in a hiding place all three know of and invites them to live with her. Write and change lines to explain all this. If you are a hard-hearted traditionalist, the Wolf can eat Pigs 1 and 2, and the Wolf can die in a pot of boiling water.

Set

Decorate the stage front with trees, bushes, grass, flowers, brooks, etc. to suggest a country setting. Leave the playing area clear so that all the action is clearly visible. While there are many props, they can be simply produced.

Cut pieces of brown and yellow construction paper into narrow strips and tie them together with string or thread. They make fine bundles of straw and sticks. Make houses two- or three-dimensional by gluing the strips onto a house shape. The load of bricks is represented by a rectangular shape, two- or three-dimensional, of red construction paper with lines suggesting the shape of bricks drawn on it. Simple drawings on yellow, brown, and red construction paper will be fine as well. Reinforce two-dimensional houses with rulers or dowels taped to the back. A handle on the bottom allows the puppeteer or prop handler to move it up onto the stage and off when it is blown down. Cut a small window. Draw a door on the house that does not open.

The pigs enter the house by going below stage and coming up into the house from below. This break in realism is not significant. If your puppets cannot handle props, put the bundles of straw, sticks, and bricks on small platforms with handles or dowels underneath and have a prop person move them around with the appropriate puppet.

Action

The Pig-Wolf chase scenes can go on as long as the ingenuity of the puppeteers and the interest of the audience hold out. Move the puppets in a fast sweeping action alternating with quick side-to-side jerks and looks backward for the Pigs and long, low leaps for the Wolf. Slide whistles and lots of screaming accompany this action. If you want to use recorded music, chase music from silent movies is great.

Program Building

Library Programs

Puppets can recite poems and nursery rhymes about pigs. *Stories:* "The Old Woman and Her Pig" is a good flannel board story. *Read Aloud:* "The Amazing Pig" or "Pig's Picnic." *Book Talk:* Display and introduce some books on wolves. *Music:* "There Was an Old Woman and She Had a Little Pig." *Short Craft:* Make a simple wolf paper-bag puppet.

Classroom Study Units:

Besides the play production itself, other areas of exploration are suggested by the story of "The Three Pigs." The history of mankind's relationship with wolves (and other predators) is one. Collect pig stories and pig books. Learn about varieties of wild and domestic pigs. Using the pig houses as a beginning point, explore how animals build houses. Why do they build them the ways they do? For art projects make pig and wolf paper bag puppets and surround masks. Make a village of piggy houses made of straw, sticks, leaves, corn cobs, newspapers, cans, or any found objects.

Bibliography

Picture Books

The Amazing Bone. William Steig. Farrar, Straus and Giroux, 1976. (1–3)

The Amazing Pig. Paul Galdone. Houghton Mifflin, 1981. (K–3)

Chester the Worldly Pig. Bill Peet. Houghton Mifflin, 1965. (K–3)

Farmer Mack Measures his Pig. Tony Johnston. Harper Row, 1986. (4–6)

The First Dog. Jan Brett. Harcourt Brace Jovanovich, 1988. (P–1)

The Gunniwolf. Wilhelmina Harper. Dutton, 1967. (P–K)

Perfect Pig: An Introduction to Manners. Marc Tolon Brown. Little Brown, 1983. (K–2)

Pig Pig Grows Up. David McPhail. Dutton, 1980. (P–1)

The Pig's Picnic. Keiko Kasza. Putnam, 1988. (P–2)

A Treeful of Pigs. Arnold Lobel. Greenwillow, 1979. (K–2)

The Wolf's Chicken Stew. Keiko Kasza. Putnam, 1987. (P–K)

Zeke Pippin. William Steig. Harper Collins, 1994 (1–3)

Longer Fiction

Babe the Gallant Pig. Dick King-Smith. Crown, 1985. (4–5)

Charlotte's Web. E. B. White. Harper Collins, 1974. (3–6)

Freddy and the Perilous Adventure. Walter R. Brooks. Knopf, 1986. (3–5) (Series)

Nonfiction:

And So They Build. Bert Kitchen. Candlewick, 1993. (K–3)

Animal Architects. Donald Crump. National Geographic, 1987. (3–5)

Animal Homes. Illa Podendorf. Children's Press, 1982. (1–4)

Fur, Feathers, and Flippers: How Animals Live Where They Do. Patricia Lauber. Scholastic, 1994. (3–5)

Homes: How Animals Find Comfort and Safety. Macmillan, 1987. (3–7)

The Kingdom of Wolves. Scott Barry. Putnam, 1979. (4–6)

Wolf Tracks: Tracking Wolves in the Wild. Sylvia A. Johnson. Learner, 1985. (5–8)

Wolfman: Exploring the World of Wolves. Laurence Pringle. Macmillan, 1983. (5–8)

The Wonder of Wolves: A Story and Activities. Sandra Chisholm Robinson. Roberts Rinehart, 1989. (3–6)

Songs

"There Was an Old Woman and She Had a Little Pig." *Animal Folk Songs For Children.* Ruth Crawford Seeger. Doubleday, 1948. (2–6)

11

Too Much Noise

Performers: grades 4 through 8
Audience: preschool through grade 2

Cast: Narrator
Farmer
Wife
Wise Woman
Cow
Pig
Donkey
Dog
Cat
Chickens, ducks, geese

Props: Baby.

Set: Rural farmhouse stage left, Wise Woman's house on far stage right. An artist's easel is set up next to house.

Narrator Enters stage right and moves to center stage:

Narrator: Once upon a time a farmer lived in a little house with his wife and their baby daughter. His wife was a cheerful person. As she worked around their home,

101

dusting and stirring pots of soup, she held their baby and sang to her. The baby laughed and babbled, but sometimes, like all babies, the baby cried. That farmer wanted silence in his home. He worked hard on his farm and he wanted peace. Also, he was grumpy. These happy sounds irritated him. So you see, he was a foolish man as well as a grumpy one. This is what happened.

Exit Narrator stage right, then enter Wise Woman stage right. The woman turns to easel, her back to stage left, and begins painting. Enter wife stage left holding baby and humming. Farmer enters center stage, crosses to stage left, and falls asleep, leaning over the edge of the stage. He is snoring loudly.

Wife: "Oh, who built the ark? Noah, Noah. Noah built the ark".

Baby: Noah, Noah!

Farmer: Wakes up. What? Why must this house be so noisy?

Wife: Poor dear dumpling! Never mind. Our supper is ready now.

Farmer: Never mind? I work hard in the fields all day. Can't I have a little nap when I get home?

Wife: Yes, dear, but it is time to eat now.

Baby: Wah, wah, wah.

Wife: There, there, little pigeon. You mustn't shout, dear, it upsets her.

Farmer: Upset! Upset! I'll tell you who is upset!

Wife: Now my dear, my sweet honey cake, calm yourself. I have an idea. I know the noise of our home is difficult for you. In the village there is a very wise woman. Everyone has been going to her for advice—when to plant potatoes, when to pick apples, whom to marry, how to cure stomach ache, all kinds of problems. Now I am sure that if you go to her, she will find a way for you be happy with our home.

Farmer: Great! I will go now. I'll eat later. *Farmer goes to stage right to Wise Woman.*

Farmer: Good evening, Wise Woman. I hope you are well.

Wise Woman: Turns to face farmer. Well enough. And you?

Farmer: I am well—no, I am troubled. My wife tells me you have good advice to share. My home is unbearably noisy. My wife sings constantly as she works, and my baby laughs and giggles and even cries. What am I to do? I work hard on my farm. I need peace.

Wise Woman: Ah, yes. That is a serious problem. My, my, my. Hmmm. Tell me, do you have a cow on your farm?

Farmer: Yes, a fine black and white cow. Why?

Wise Woman: You must go home and take that cow from the pasture and put it in your house. Then your problem with noise will be over.

Farmer: But—well, I guess, if you're sure, Wise Woman. Good evening.

Wise Woman: Give my best wishes to your wife, Farmer. *Turns to easel while Farmer goes to center stage.*

Farmer: This is strange advice, but she is a Wise Woman after all. Bossy? Bossy? Come here, girl—come along here.

Cow enters center stage from below and approaches Farmer.
Cow: Moo?

Farmer leads Cow as far left as possible into house. Cow moos questioningly over and over, and then angrily after she is in house.

Farmer: Hello, my dear. The Wise Woman said to bring our Cow into the house to help solve the noise problem.

Wife: Oh. That's a fine idea. Hello, Bossy. Say hello to the cow, my little musk melon. *Shows baby to Cow.*

Baby: Goo, goo. Moo.

Wife: Sings." "I had a cow and the cow pleased me and I fed my cow under yonder tree, and the cow said . . ."

Cow: Moo! Moo! *Continually until farmer leaves.*

Baby: Moo moo, goo goo. *Continually until farmer leaves.*

Farmer: I don't think this is working. I'm going back to the Wise Woman. Perhaps I did something wrong. *Farmer moves stage right.*

Wise Woman: Turns from easel. Hello again, Farmer.

Farmer: Wise Woman, something is wrong. I brought the Cow into my house, but now it is noisier than ever. What shall I do?

Wise Woman: Hmmm. Perhaps the Cow isn't enough to solve your problem. Do you have a donkey on your farm?

Farmer: Yes, I do.

Wise Woman: Well, put the donkey in your house beside the Cow. That should fix things.

Farmer: Oh, all right. Ummm, thank you, Wise Woman.

Farmer goes to center stage.

Farmer: Hector! Come here, old boy!

Donkey comes from below center stage and approaches Farmer.

Donkey: Hee haw!

Farmer: There you are, old friend. Now you won't understand this, but I am going to take you into the house.

Donkey: Distressed. Hee haw, hee haw, hee haw. *Farmer leads donkey into house next to Cow.*

Wife: Hector! Hello, Hector. Let me get some oats for you.

Farmer: The Wise Woman said to bring Hector into the house too. She said the Cow wasn't enough to fix the noise problem.

Cow: Moo, moo, moo.

Hector: Hee haw, hee haw, hee haw.

Baby: Wah, wah, wah, wah.

Wife: Sings. "Hush Little Baby." *All four sing continually until Farmer leaves.*

Farmer: Groans. I'm going back to the Wise Woman's house. Something is wrong with this plan. *Farmer moves stage right.*

Farmer: Uh, Wise Woman. I have done just what you said to do. The Cow and the Donkey are in the house. But, you see, there is more noise than ever. Perhaps you made a mistake.

Wise Woman: Oh no, I never make mistakes. It takes a little experimentation to get the plan just right. Apparently a cow and a donkey are not enough in your case. Do you have any dogs?

Farmer: Groan. Yes, I have two. Nano and Nanette. They help herd the sheep.

Wise Woman: Ah. Well that is very good. Go home and take Nano and Nanette into your house. And take the sheep in also, just for good measure. That should do it.

Farmer: Yes, Wise Woman, I will do that. *Head hanging.* Whatever you say. *Goes to center stage.*

Farmer: Nano, Nanette! *Whistles.* Good dogs.

Dogs: Whine, whimper.

Farmer: Get the sheep and drive them into the house. Into the house! Go get em!

Dogs: Bark?

Dogs dash off and return stage right, driving sheep stage left and barking wildly. The sheep are "baaing." All enter house and move stage left. There is continuous barking, baaing, mooing, hee-hawing, and crying continually until Farmer leaves.

Wife: Shouting. Hello dear. I think things are improving a bit. That Wise Woman certainly knows what she is doing.

Farmer: Shouting. What? I can't hear you! Oh, never mind! *Moves to stage right.*

Farmer: Wise Woman, I have no animals left but chickens, ducks, and geese.

Wise Woman: Well, you know what to do.

Farmer: Ohhh! *Goes to center stage.* Here chick, chick, chick. Here Chick, chick, chick.

Chickens, ducks, and geese gather from below center stage and Farmer drives them into house. All animals make noise. Baby is crying, wife singing "There's No Place Like Home." "Farmer breaks down crying, then moves stage right.

Farmer: Oh Wise Woman, in my effort to make my home quiet, I've made it impossible. It's so noisy. I can't hear my wife sing or my baby laugh.

Wise Woman: Well, my cure has worked then! Go home and put the chickens, geese, and ducks out into the yard.

Farmer: Yes, Wise Woman.

Farmer goes home and shoos chickens, etc., out. They cluck, honk, and quack as they disappear below stage level.

Farmer: To Wise Woman. The birds are out.

Wise Woman: Now the dogs and the sheep!!

Farmer: Dogs and sheep. Right. *Drives them out of the house and offstage with much barking and baaing.* The dogs and the sheep are out!

Wise Woman: The Donkey is next.

Farmer: Out you go, Donkey. *Donkey moves out of house and offstage with much hee hawing.* The Donkey is history!

Wise Woman: It's the Cow's turn!

Farmer: Got it! Bye bye, Bossy. There's some great grass down the hill there. *Cow goes offstage with much mooing.*

Wife: My goodness.

Farmer: Little mustard spoon, I am so sorry to have been such a grump. I love your singing. I love the baby's laughing and cooing and even her crying. I am going to go thank the Wise Woman for her help, and then I want you to teach me that song about Old MacDonald, the farmer.

Farmer moves stage right.

Farmer: To Wise Woman. Thank you. I am wiser now, and happier!

Wise Woman: Oh, it was nothing. Tell your wife to come for tea tomorrow, and bring the baby too. Oh, boys and girls, our play is over, so clap and cheer and make too much noise. The end.

Playing Notes

Puppets and Puppeteers

Classroom or Workshop Production

If you are performing this play with many puppeteers, you can have as many animals as you have puppets and room backstage. With carefully worked-out crowd control backstage, you could have enough animals to make a mighty din. The animals must respond to signals to be silent or to make noise so that the lines of the human puppets can be heard. Feel free to change the animals to suit the puppets you have, but remember to change the lines to reflect the puppet changes. A charming effect is achieved if animals are played by children wearing surround masks and face paint. After the play is over, the puppet cast sings "Old MacDonald" with the Wise Woman as conductor.

Library Production

This play can be performed by two puppeteers and a helper, but more is better to make the greatest amount of noise. Eliminate or add animals to suit your puppet collection and staff. The animals are moved by the helper. Put your animal puppets on rods and rig up a stand to hold them inside the Farmer's house to free the puppeteers' hands. The Wise Woman puppeteer and the helper can be animal voices. The Mother puppet holds the Baby at all times, so no separate Baby puppeteeer is needed as the Mother puppeteer makes the Baby noises. Since the animals simply make animal noises and only move onto the stage, into the house, and then out of the house and offstage, you may be able to recruit helpers from the staff, patrons (adult or child) who look cooperative, or even the audience. Invite the audience to join in the animal noises in any case. The types and numbers of animals can be changed to suit the types of animal puppets you have. Use full-face animal masks if that is more comfortable for volunteers.

Props and Scenery

The front of the stage is decorated with cutouts of farmyard tools, a barn, chicken coop, wind-

mill, fruit trees, piles of hay, etc. A large part of stage left must be set apart as the Farmer's house so that all the animals will fit in. Place cutouts of furniture below the playing level on the front surface of your theater. Add curtains on one side and drape a piece of cloth suggesting a rug over the playing area in the Farmer's house to suggest a humble dwelling. The Wise Woman does not really need a house. Drape another "rug" over the edge of the playing area where she sits. The Wise Woman should have something to occupy her when she is not giving advice. I like the choice of paintbrush and easel. You could use whatever suits your fancy or happens to be in your store of props.

Program Building

Library Program

If you will need members of the audience to be the animals, select them at the start of the program and send them backstage to be coached by one of the puppeteers. Tell a story while the volunteers are being coached. *Story:* "Great Big Enormous Turnip" (audience helps with pulling). *Read Aloud:* "Soup from a Nail" or "Stone Soup." *Short Craft:* Make cow, donkey, sheep, or dog hats by attaching paper ears and horns to strips of paper that are stapled into rings to fit children's heads. *Music:* "Old MacDonald Had a Farm."

Longer Programs and Projects

"Too Much Noise" is a Jewish story, sometimes called "It Could Always Be Worse." In many versions, the Wise Woman is a male rabbi. You could change the puppet character to a rabbi if you wish. There are many, many wonderful and hilarious Jewish stories, and many have been collected in books for children. It is a rich tradition, full of humor and joy in the simple things of life, and offers gentle lessons on the importance of paying attention to life's truths.

The production of this play could be part of a classroon unit on values: their differences and similarities in various cultures and how they are presented in folk literature. *Aesop's Fables* might be introduced as an example of another type of morality tale. Find other stories from different cultures that are used as teaching tales. Discuss stories as a way of teaching. For older children, "Too Much Noise" might be part of a unit on the Holocaust, helping students understand the significance of that tragedy by imparting a little of the value and flavor of the community that was so nearly destroyed. It might also make that knowledge easier for children (and adults) to comprehend and bear.

Bibliography

Picture Books

Beats Me Claude. Joan Lowery Nixon. Viking Kestrel, 1986. (2–4)

Farmer Palmer's Wagon Ride. William Steig. Farrar, Straus and Giroux, 1974. (2–4)

Great Big Enormous Turnip. Alexkaey Tolstoy. F. Walker, 1968. (K–2)

It Could Always Be Worse: A Yiddish Folktale. Margot Zemach. Farrar, Straus and Giroux, 1976. (K–3)

Just Enough Is Plenty: A Hanukkah Tale. Barbara Goldini. Viking, 1988. (K–3)

McBroom and the Great Race. Sid Fleischman. Little, Brown, 1980. (K–4)

My Noah's Ark. M. B. Goffstein. Harper and Row, 1978. (P–3)

Stone Soup. Ann Mcgovern. Scholastic, 1986. (K–3)

Stone Soup. Marcia Brown. Macmillan, 1982. (1–4)

Too Much Noise. Ann Mcgovern. Houghton Mifflin, 1967. (K–3)

Longer Fiction

Island on Bird Street. Uri Orlevr. Houghton Mifflin, 1984. (5–9)

Night Journey. Kathryn Lasky. Puffin, 1988. (5–9)

Number the Stars. Lois Lowry. Dell, 1990. (4–7)

The Return. Sonia Levitin. Fawcett, 1987. (6–10)

Upstairs Room. Johanna Reiss. Harper Collins, 1987. (5–10)

When Hitler Stole Pink Rabbit. Judith Kerr. Dell, 1987. (4–7)

Story Collections

The Feather Merchants and Other Tales of the Fools of Chelm. Steve Sanfield. Morrow. 1993. (3–6)

Let's Steal the Moon: Jewish Tales, Ancient and Recent. Blanche Serwer-Bernstein. Shapolsky, 1970. (7 and up)

Zlateh the Goat. I. B. Singer. Harper and Row, 1984. (3–12) (All Singer collections and titles)

Nonfiction

A Day of Pleasure: Stories of a Boy Growing Up in Warsaw. I. B. Singer. Farrar, Straus and Giroux, 1986. (4–12)

The Jewish Kids Catalog. Chaya M. Burstein. Jewish Publication Society of America, 1993. (K–8)

The Jewish World. Douglas Charing. Silver, 1984. (3–6)

Judaism. Myer Domnitz. Watts, 1986. (4–6)

Never to Forget: The Jews of the Holocaust. Milton Meltzer. Harper and Row, 1976. (6–12)

A Nightmare in History: The Holocaust. Miriam Chaikim. Clarion, 1987. (5–10)

Rescue: The Story of How Gentiles Saved Jews in the Holocaust. Milton Metzler. Harper and Row, 1988. (6–12)

We Remember the Holocaust. David Adler. Holt, 1989. (5–12)

The Rise of Modern Religions. Georgia Makhlouf. Silver. 1988. (5–8)

World of Our Fathers. Milton Meltzer. Farrar, Straus and Giroux. 1974. (6–adult)

Cookbooks

The Children's Jewish Holiday Kitchen. Joan Nathan. Schocken, 1987. (K–6)

Poetry

Poems for Jewish Holidays. Myra Cohen Livingston. Holiday House, 1986 (3–8)

12
Wiley and the Hairy Man

Performers: grades 5 through 8
Audience: kindergarten through grade 3

Cast: Wiley
      Momma, Wiley's mother
      Hairy Man
      Dog(s)
      Pig(s)
      Dinosaur
      Elephant
      Mouse

Props: Ax, ropes, coil of rope at Wiley's waist, cloth sack, blanket.

Set: Rural scene. A cabin stage right with a porch in front and a clothes line coming from the back and ending at a pole or small tree. A large tree stage left with moss hanging from branches.

Wiley and Momma on porch.

Wiley: Ma, I'm going to go to the swamp to cut some bamboo poles. I'm taking my ax. Okay?

Momma: Now Wiley, you listen to me. I know all about that swamp: it can be a dangerous place. The Hairy Man likes to roam in there, and he is as scary as any monster. He will get you if you don't watch out. Take your hound dogs with you. The Hairy Man hates hound dogs. And remember this—he has feet like a cow, so he can't climb trees. If you want to get away from him, climb a tree. I know all about the Hairy Man.

Wiley: I'll watch out, Momma. I'll take my hound dogs with me everywhere I go. Come on, you dogs. Let's go. We're not afraid of any old Hairy Man.

Mother exits into cabin stage right. Wiley moves stage right, one third of way. Dogs see pig.

Pig: Oink, oink, oink.

Pig moves stage right and offstage. Dogs rush offstage right past cabin, barking and chasing pig.

Wiley: Hey, dogs. Come back here, dogs. Come back. Oh well. Those dogs have gone off so far I can't even hear them anymore. Sure hope that Hairy Man isn't around. *To audience.* Boys and girls, I might need your help. If I say, "I hear my dogs coming," you bark and bark like you're all a bunch of dogs. Okay? Do you want to practice? Okay. *Audience barks.* Great! Good barking!

Wiley looks around and moves stage left. Enter the Hairy Man popping up from behind the tree stage left, to the left of the tree. Wiley sees him.

Wiley: Oh, no! It's the Hairy Man! Oooh, is he ugly: green hair all over him, big slobbery teeth, shiny red eyes. Yuck! Good thing that old Hairy Man has feet like a cow and cannot climb trees.

Wiley climbs the tree on the backstage side. His ax accidentally falls to the foot of the tree on the right.

Hairy Man: Wiley. *Sweetly.* Wiley. *Moves to right side of tree.* What are you doing up in that tree?

Wiley: My mother told me to stay away from you.

Hairy Man: Me? Sweet little old me? Why, I'm just an ordinary old Hairy Man.

110

Wiley: Well, what've you got that sack for, hmm?

Hairy Man: Oh, nothing. Heh, heh, heh. Oh look, an ax. Does this belong to you, Wiley? I think I will just cut down this tree you're in. *Makes motions of chopping down tree, and pieces or chips fly from the tree onto the ground.*

Wiley: Oh no! The Hairy Man is chopping down my tree. Wait! I remember some magic my Momma told me about. I will just use my Momma's magic! Fly chips fly, back in your same old place! *Chips fly back on to the tree trunk.*

Hairy Man: Grrr. The chips of wood are flying right back into the trunk of the tree. The chips are filling in the chops. I will just have to chop faster. *Chop, chop, chop.*

Wiley: Fly chips fly, back in your same old place! *Chips fly back again.*

Hairy Man: Pant, pant. I'm not getting anywhere. That Momma magic is powerful. As fast as I chop away this tree, the chips go flying back and fill up the chops.

Wiley: Wait, Hairy Man, I think I hear my dogs coming.

Dogs bark wildly offstage and children bark in audience.

Hairy Man: Whines and whimpers. I do not like dogs. They scare me. I'm out of here—I'm history. Bye!.

Hairy Man exits stage left. Dogs enter stage right, barking and jumping near tree. Wiley gets down from tree.

Wiley: Come on, you dogs. Let's go home and tell Momma about this. *Runs home, stage right.*

Wiley: Momma, Momma. I saw the Hairy Man.

Momma: Enters stage right. Did the Hairy Man try to get you?

Wiley: Yes, Ma'am, he did.

Momma: Well, the next time that old Hairy Man comes after you, do not climb a tree. Just stay on the ground and say, "Hello, Hairy Man." The Hairy Man will say "Hello, Wiley." Then you say, "I hear you are the best conjure man around here."

Wiley: What's a conjure man, Momma?

Momma: It means a magician. You tell him he is the best conjure man. He'll say, "I reckon I am." Then you say, "I bet you can't change yourself into an elephant." And he will.

Wiley: Really?

Momma: Yes. He will change himself into an elephant. Then you say, "I bet you can't change into a dinosaur. And he will change himself into a dinosaur. You keep telling him what he can't do and he'll keep doing it—just to show you. Then you say "Everybody can change into something big. I bet you can't change yourself into something little—like a mouse. That Hairy Man will change himself into a little mouse. You grab him right away and throw him into the river.

Wiley: Okay, Momma. I'm going right back to the swamp to get those bamboo poles. *Defiantly.* That Hairy Man better leave me alone. Think I'll tie these dogs up so they don't run after any more pigs. *Ties up dogs by laying rope over their necks.*

Dogs: Whimper, whimper.

Wiley: Hush, dogs.

Wiley goes to center stage, then Hairy Man enters stage left and they meet.

Hairy Man: Hi, Wiley. Heh heh. Where are your dogs? Heh, heh.

Wiley: Oh, they're at home. Hey, Hairy Man, I hear you are the best conjure man around here.

Hairy Man: You bet I am. I am the best hairy conjure man in the world.

Wiley: I bet you can't change yourself into an elephant.

Hairy Man: An elephant? Ho, ho. Sure can. Easiest thing in the world. *Whistle.* There!

Elephant appears from below as Hairy Man disappears.

Wiley: Oh my. It is an elephant! Bet you can't change yourself into a dinosaur.

Hairy Man: As elephant. Dinosaur? Almost as easy as an elephant. *Whistle.*

Dinosaur appears from below as elephant disappears.

Hairy Man: As dinosaur. What's next, Wiley, a dragon, hm? How about a dragon? That's pretty flashy. *Changes into dragon.*

Wiley: Well, gee. Anybody can change himself into a big thing. Can you change yourself into something small—like a mouse?

Hairy Man: No problem. *Whistle.* There. *Mouse appears.*

Wiley: Aha! Gott cha, Hairy Man. Guess you are not the best conjure man after all. Ha. *Grabs mouse and throws it behind stage.* It's into the river with you, Hairy Man. Now, I will just get those bamboo poles and go home.
Wiley moves stage left. Hairy Man appears behind Wiley.

Hairy Man: Singsong. Oh Wiley, hello.

Wiley: Gasp! *Climbs tree.* How did you get out of the river, Hairy Man?

Hairy Man: I changed myself into the wind and blew my way out. Told you I was the world's greatest conjure man. Now I am going to wait right here until you get hungry and come down out of that tree. I could use a little nap.*Lies down.*

Wiley: Hmm. Hairy Man?

Hairy Man: Snoring. Humph, humph. What?

Wiley: Hairy Man, you did some pretty good animal tricks, but I bet you can't make ordinary things, like rope, disappear.

Hairy Man: Things? Things? Why they're much easier than animal tricks. I could make all the rope in this county disappear! *Raises hand and a whistle sounds.* All the rope in this county—disappear!

All ropes disappear. Wiley's rope disappears. Clothesline at Wiley's house falls down, the rope holding the dogs disappears, and the dogs are free.
Wiley: My dogs are free! I hear my dogs coming. I hear my dogs coming.

Dogs bark and head for Wiley, moving stage left and barking.

Wiley: Here dogs, here dogs.

Hairy Man: Oh no, oh no, dogs—I hate dogs. EEEE! *Exit Hairy Man stage left.*

Wiley: Comes down from tree. Come on dogs, let's go home. We need Momma's help. *Wiley and dogs go home, stage right.*

Wiley: Momma, I met that old Hairy Man again, and I fooled him again.

Momma: Enters stage right: Well, you fooled the Hairy Man twice. If we can fool him one more time, he will never come back to bother us again. If you trick him three times he has to leave you alone forever. But it's mighty hard to fool the Hairy

Man three times. Let's give this some thought.

Wiley and Momma and dogs put their hands to their heads.

Momma: Wiley, go down to the pen and bring me back a little pig. I'm going to put the dogs in the barn so the Hairy Man won't be afraid to come by.

Wiley and Momma exit stage right leading dogs. Dogs whimper and cry from back- stage. Mother and Wiley come back stage right. Momma has a blanket, and Wiley has a little pig.

Pig: Oink, oink, oink, oink.

Wiley: Here's the pig, Momma.

Momma: Now let's put that little piglet down on the porch, and you go hide.

Wiley puts pig down and hides stage right behind cabin. He can be seen peeking around the corner of the cabin. Dogs howl and cry offstage.

Momma: Hush, you dogs! You'll scare the Hairy Man off and spoil everything. *She covers pig with blanket and sings.* "Hush little baby, don't say a word, Momma's gonna buy you a mockingbird" la, la, la, la, la hmm, hmm, hmmm . . .

Hairy Man enters stage left and moves quickly across stage to cabin, stage right, grunt- ing, snorting, and harrumphing when he sees Momma.

Momma: Hello, Hairy Man.

Hairy Man: Momma, I've come for your young 'un.

Momma: You can't have him, Hairy Man!

Hairy Man: If you don't give him to me, I'll set your house on fire with lightning.

Momma: I have plenty of sweet milk, Hairy Man. The milk will put out the fire.

Hairy Man: I'll dry up your cow. I'll dry up your spring. I'll send a million boll weevils out of the ground to eat up your cotton if you don't give me your young 'un.

Momma: Hairy Man, you wouldn't do all that. That's mighty mean.

Hairy Man: Well I'm a mighty mean and hairy man. Roar! Roar!

Momma: Eek! If I do give you the young 'un, will you go away and never come back? Pleeeease, Mr. Hairy Man?

Hairy Man: I promise I will—cross my heart and hope to die.

Momma: Sobs. There's my young 'un, over there. *Points to pig.* Boo, hoo, hoo, hoo. *Covers eyes.*

Hairy Man: Heh, heh, heh. *Picks up pig.* Hey . . . this is a pig. I want that Wiley boy. *Drops pig.*

Pig: Oink, oink, oink, oink!

Momma: It's a young pig. Ha ha, I never said which young 'un I'd give you.

Hairy Man: Roar! Roar! Gnash! Snarl! Aaargh! Growl! Boo hoo.

Dogs begin to bark. Hairy Man runs away, crying, exits stage left.

Momma: Come on out, Wiley. That Hairy Man is gone for good. We fooled him three times. He can't ever come back here again, and he can't ever get us.

Wiley enters stage right and hugs Momma.

Wiley: My mother is the best conjure woman in the world!!!

Dogs return, are petted, and bark.

Wiley and Momma: The end.

Playing Notes

Puppeteers and Puppets

In addition to using one puppeteer for each character, more dogs and pigs can be added. This play is based on an African-American story, so Wiley and his mother should be African-American puppets. The Hairy Man can be any puppet with lots of green hair added. He can change into larger creatures or smaller creatures, getting smaller and smaller until the mouse appears. Use the animal puppets you have on hand and improvise animal sounds to enliven their appearance. Put a large tuft of green hair on each animal puppet so that the connection with the Hairy Man is reinforced. Be sure to change Wiley's and the Hairy Man's lines to match your puppets. You will need prop and sound managers for the rope trips, the chopping trick and associated noises, as well as the animal noises.

Library Production

Two puppeteers and a helper can perform this play if the numbers of dogs and pigs are reduced to one each. One puppeteer is Wiley and Wiley's mother. The other puppeteer is the Hairy Man and the dog. Put the pig, elephant, dinosaur, and mouse puppets on rods to be manipulated by the helper. The helper must also make the ropes disappear and make the chips fly off and back onto the tree. Very few script changes are required, so a shorter version is not included.

Props and Scenery

Decorate the stage front as a southern rural scene. On the cabin side add rows of crops, a small plow, chicken coops, etc. Attach a clothes line to the back side of the cabin with clothes hanging from it. On the swamp side add grasses, bushes, cutouts of swamp animals, and cypress trees.

The tree is an important piece of scenery in the swamp. It must be wide enough so that the puppeteer's hand is mostly hidden as Wiley climbs it. The chips that fly off and back onto the tree as the Hairy Man chops are located near the roots at the base of the tree. Cut one or two grooves into the edge of the tree in this area so that the chips can be attached there. Using the same material you used to make the tree, cut irregularly shaped pieces of bark and add small rods to the back side. The prop manager or helper lifts them up and off the tree and then puts them back, resting the rod in the grooves, one at a time. If you want to simplify the production, one chip is enough to create the illusion. Small bits of cheesecloth colored lightly with a black felt marker and hung in the branches of the tree make excellent Spanish moss.

There are three parts to the illusion that the Hairy Man makes all the ropes disappear. The clothes line falls down, the dog's rope flies off the dog's collar, and the coil of rope hanging at Wiley's waist flies away. Attach strong buttonhole thread or transparent fish line to the ends of the dog's rope and Wiley's rope so that the rope can be jerked off and appear to fly away. The clothesline is attached at either end by Velcro or some other temporary means so that it can be jerked free.

Action

Wiley's Mother is very calm and self-confident. Wiley is respectful and courageous. The Hairy Man is blustery, bouncy, loud, and continually in motion. His magic is accompanied by leaps and bounces and throwing his arms out. His cries of rage and fear are loud. He chuckles and laughs when he seems to be winning, whines and sobs when losing. Coach the children in the audience to bark with the dogs, but you will want to have a signal for them to stop barking. Practice removing the chips from the tree and replacing them many times. The trick with the ropes must be practiced many times until it works perfectly, first Wiley's rope, then the clothes line, and last of all the dogs' rope. Do the tricks slowly so that the action is not over before the audience has caught on to what is happening. When Wiley's mother tricks the Hairy Man with the pig, simply lay the pig puppet's head on the stage's front edge and place a blanket over it. It begins oinking loudly after the Hairy Man discovers he has been tricked.

Program Building

Library Programs

This play is an excellent centerpiece for a Black History Month program. There are many, many African and African-American stories and songs that would complete the program. It is a good play for Halloween programs as well. *Read Aloud:* "Anansi and the Talking Melons," "Abiyoyo," or "Mirandy and Brother Wind." *Stories:* "The Rabbit and the Well," "Why Men Have to Work," or "Why Sun and Moon Live in the Sky." *Music:* "Abiyoyo." *Short Craft:* Make a collage picture of the Hairy Man. Have plenty of "green hair" available to complete the picture.

Longer Programs and Classroom Units

Wiley and the Hairy Man would work well as part of a classroom unit on black history. Enrich units on the Civil War with information on slavery and the economy of the South. The huge, rich body of folk tales from Africa is a wonderful heritage that all children deserve to know. Trace the roots of folk tales using maps of Africa, the United States, and Central and South America.

Bibliography

Picture Books

Abiyoyo. Pete Seeger. Simon and Schuster, 1994. (P–1)

Anansi and the Talking Melons. Eric Kimel. Holiday House, 1994. (K–2)

A Chair for my Mother. Vera B. William. Greenwillow, 1982. (K–2)

Cherries and Cherry Pits. Vera B. Williams. Greenwillow, 1982. (K–2)

How Many Stars in the Sky. Lenny Hirt. Tambourine, 1991. (K–1)

Jafta and the Wedding. Hugh Lewin. Carolrhoda, 1983. (P–2)

Mirandy and Brother Wind. Patricia McKissack. Knopf, 1988. (K–3)

The Patchwork Quilt. Valerie Flournoy. Dial, 1985. (2–4)

Peter's Chair. Ezra Jack Keats. Harper and Row, 1967. (P–K) (All Keats)

Tar Beach. Faith Ringgold. Crown, 1991. (K–2)

Longer Fiction

Drinking Gourd. F. N. Monjo. Harper and Row, 1970. (2–4)

House of Dies Drear. Virginia Hamilton. Macmillan, 1968. (5–8)

Justin and the Best Biscuits in the World. Mildred P. Taylor. Lothrop, 1986 (2–5)

Long Journey Home. Julius Lester. Dial, 1972. (6–9)

Me, Mop, and the Moondance Kid. Walter Dean Myers. Delacorte, 1988. (3

Roll of Thunder, Hear My Cry. Mildred D. Taylor. Dial, 1976. (5–8)

Secret of Gumbo Grove. Eleanora Tate. Watts, 1987. (5–8)

Shimmershine Queens. Camille Yarbrough. Putnam, 1989. (5–8)

Something Upstairs. Avi. Watts, 1988. (5–7)

The Stories Julian Tells. Ann Cameron. Pantheon Books, 1981. (1–3)

Stories

Adventures of High John the Conqueror. Steve Sanfield. Orchard Books, 1985. (6–8) *Black Folktales:* Julius Lester. Grove Press, 1970. (3–8).

The Dark Thirty: Southern Tales of the Supernatural. Patricia McKissack. Knopf, 1992. (4–8)

Knee High Man and Other Tales. Julius Lester. Dial, 1972. (2–5)

Mufaro's Beautiful Daughters. John Steptoe. Lothrop, 1987. (1–4)

The People Could Fly: American Black Folktales. Virginia Hamilton. Knopf, 1985. (3–8)

Raw Head, Bloody Bones: African American Tales of the Supernatural. Mary Lyins. Scribners, 1991. (5–8)

The Tales of Uncle Remus: The Adventures of Brer Rabbit. Julius Lester. Dial, 1987. (4–8)

The Talking Eggs: A Folktale From the American South. Robert D. San Souci. Dial, 1989. (2–4)

Chapter 12

Nonfiction

All Times, All Peoples: A World History of Slavery. Milton Meltzer. Harper and Row, 1980. (4–8)

Frederick Douglass: In His Own Words. Milton Meltzer. Harcourt Brace Jovanavich, 1994. (6–12)

Frederick Douglass: The Black Lion. Patricia McKissack. Children's, 1985. (4–6)

Freedom Rides. James Haskins. Hyperion, 1994. (4–8)

Go Free or Die. A Story About Harriet Tubman. Jeri Ferris. Carolrhoda, 1988. (3–6)

Harriet Tubman. Anne Perry. Crowell, 1955 (5–8)

Life and Death of Martin Luther King Jr. James Haskins. Lothrop, 1977. (5–7)

Malcolm X. Arnold Adoff. Harper amd Row, 1970. (3–5)

Martin Luther King, Jr.: Free at Last. David Adler. Holiday House, 1985. (3–6)

Mary McLeod Bethune: A Great American. Patricia McKissack. Children's Press, 1985. (4–6)

Step It Down. Bessie Jones. University of Georgia Press, 1987 . (K–adult)

Shake It to the One That You Love Best. Cheryl Warren Mattox. Warren Mattox Productions, 1989. (K–5)

Media

African Story Journey (video recording). Susan Saltz. Churchill Media, 1992.

Brer Rabbit Stories Told by Jackie Torrence (sound recording). Weston Woods, 1984.

I'm Gonna Let It Shine (sound recording). Bill Harley. Round River Records, 1990.

Still on the Journey (sound recording). Sweet Honey in the Rock. Earth Beat, 1993.

Stories from the Black Tradition (video recording). Gail E. Haley and others. Weston Woods, 1992.

Appendix

Shorter Versions for Two Puppeteers and Helper

The scripts in this section are the same as those in the main section of the book except that they are shorter. Some characters are eliminated so that the play can be performed by two or three people. Performers are encouraged to make any other adjustments in the scripts that accommodate their needs and make the experience of putting on these plays fun and comfortable.

The Elf and the Shoemakers

Cast: Narrator
Husband
Wife
Elf
Little Red Riding Hood (LRRH)
Rabbit (costumed as Santa Claus)
King Balthazar

Props: Shoes, leather, bag of groceries, elf suit, and cloth for elf suit.

Set: A cobblers' shop with a Christmas tree on far stage right.

Narrator/Rabbit: Many years ago, people didn't go to stores to buy shoes, you know. All shoes were made by hand, and the people who made shoes were called shoemakers, or cobblers. Shoemakers would buy big pieces of leather, cut it into shapes, and sew the shapes into shoes. Then they would sell the shoes. There was once a husband and wife who were shoemakers. Through bad luck, they found themselves very poor. All they had left in their shop was one small piece of leather—enough to make one pair of shoes. That's where our puppet play begins, in the poor shoemaker's shop on December 21. Remember that date—December 21.

Narrator exits stage left. Enter Husband and Wife stage right.

Husband: Ah, things are not good, dear. This is all the leather we have. We can make only one more pair of shoes. I hope they are bought quickly so we can buy another bit of leather.

Wife: Don't be discouraged. Let's cut them out tonight and stitch them up tomorrow. We'll sing while we work to cheer us up.

They work, singing "We Three Kings."

Husband: "We three kings of Orient are . . ."

Wife: "Bearing gifts we travel so far, la la la, la la, . . ."

Husband: Yawning. There, that's finished.

Wife: Let's sleep now and let tomorrow bring us a new day and better luck.

Exit husband and wife stage right. Enter Elf popping up from below at stage center.

Elf: I think that these shoemakers need my help. What can I do? Aha! I could sew up these shoes while they sleep. That might make things a bit easier for them.

Sounds of tapping and hammering while Elf makes sewing and hammering motions.

Elf: Sew and sew. Tap and tap. Stitch and Stitch. And that is that. Finished. *Puts pair of shoes on counter.*

Elf: Very nice. Very, very nice. Even if I do say so myself. Time to go, bye. Good luck, shoemakers!

Elf exits with a hop up and quick sinking down at stage center.

Sign appears stage left and moves across to exit stage right. It reads "December 22." Enter shoemakers stage right.

Wife: What a fine day. Let's begin to work on the shoes.

Husband: I think it will be a lucky day. Oh, look, the leather we cut out last night has been stitched up and finished!

Wife: What tiny stitches. Why, this is very fine work.

Husband: Joking tone. Did you finish these shoes while I slept?

Wife: Of course not, you silly. You worked on them in the night, and now you're playing a trick on me.

Husband: No I didn't. *They hug.* Never mind. Here comes a customer who might buy these fine shoes.

Wife: Oh dear, it's that chatterbox, Little Red Riding Hood. I'll go get breakfast started.

Exit Wife stage right. Enter LRRH from far stage left.

LRRH: Hello, I'm Little Red Riding Hood. I am looking for some shoes for my grandmother. I think that those will do nicely. *Gestures to shoes on counter.* She hates those sensible granny shoes, you know. She like shoes with a bit of zip to them. My, my, what beautiful work. These will be perfect for Granny. You know, shoemaker, I have been wanting some red shoes to match my beautiful cape. Don't you think it's lovely? Don't I look stunning in it? Anyway, do you think you could you make me a pair of red shoes to go with my red cape?

Husband: Why, certainly. They'll be ready tomorrow afternoon.

LRRH: Very good. Here's your money. Deliver the shoes to Granny. You can't miss her house. I will tell Cinderella and everyone about your fine work. *Exit far stage left.*

Wife: Enters. Has she gone? Oh good, she bought the shoes.

Husband: Yes. She paid cash, and she ordered another pair. Let's go out and buy more leather, some red for Little Red Riding Hood, and maybe a bit of shiny black to go with the brass buckles I have been saving. And you know, I think that there will be enough money left over to buy some food for a Christmas feast.

Wife: Wonderful. We will buy figs, and nuts, and tangerines, and maybe a bit of honey.

Husband and Wife exit far stage left. Pause. Wife and Husband enter far stage left with leather and food.

Husband: Our luck is changing, I can feel it. Why, we got these pieces of leather at such a good price, there was plenty left over for food.

Wife: We will have a fine holiday feast. Only two more days until Christmas. Let's cut out the shoes tonight, and sew them in the morning.

Husband: Good idea. Just let me put these groceries away first. *Tosses bag of groceries behind Wife.* But I don't want you getting up in the night to sew them by candlelight, you silly goose.

Wife: Not me

Husband and Wife sing "We Wish You a Merry Christmas" and work on shoes.

Husband: Well—that's done. The leather is all ready to stitch. *He puts pieces of leather on counter.* Enough for three pairs of shoes. Tomorrow will be a busy day.

Husband and Wife exit stage right. Elf enters center stage as before.

Elf: Look, more shoe leather, all cut out. This red leather must be for Little Red Riding Hood. I'll just stitch them up! *Elf makes sounds of tapping and hammering.* Sew and sew, tap and tap, stitch and stitch, and that is that. All ready. *Puts shoes on counter.* Next pair! Sew and sew, tap and tap, stitch and stitch, and that is that. Wow! These are gorgeous—gold shoes! Fine enough for a king. *Puts shoes on counter.* Pair number three! Sew and sew, tap and tap, stitch and stitch, and that is that. Hmm. Shiny black boots—now who will want shiny black boots, do you suppose? *Puts shoes on counter.* Can't imagine. Oh, oh! It's time to go!

Elf exits center stage as before. Sign appears stage left and moves across to exit stage right. It reads "December 23." Enter Husband and Wife stage right.

Husband: Let's begin stitching up that leather right away. We'll begin with the red ones so that they will be finished when Little Red Riding Hood comes in.

Wife: Oh! Oh my. Look at this! All the shoes are finished. Who could have done this? And what beautiful work.

Husband: Not I! I could not stitch so fast.

Wife: And such tiny stitches. We must find out who is stitching up our shoes.

Little Red Riding Hood enters far stage left.

Husband: Here is Little Red Riding Hood for her shoes.

LRRH: Good morning, good morning. I know, I know, I'm early, but I couldn't wait to see my red shoes. Are my red shoes ready? Are they beautiful? Will they be the perfect accessory to my red cape and show off my dainty little feet? Hmmm?

Wife: Here they are, my dear. *Gestures to shoes.*

LRRH: Ooo, mmmm. They are exquisite. And don't they look nice with my cape. Everyone will admire me. Everyone will say "Who is that beautiful little girl in the red cape and red shoes?" Grandmother loved her shoes too, and now Mama wants a pair just like them, but green. Mama likes green. I like red. Here is your money. Bye. *She exits stage left taking shoes.*

Husband: How she chatters and chatters.

Wife: And how she pays! And she placed another order for more shoes. Oh dear, look down the street: It's Balthazar, one of the three kings of Orient.

Husband: Why, so it is. Heavens, could it be—he is stopping at our shop and he's coming in!

Balthazar enters far stage left.

Husband: Good morning, Sir. *He bows slightly and Balthazar bows too.*

Balthazar: Good morning. Those gold shoes. They look very, well, ah, kingly. Do they happen to be a size 12-B?

Husband: Why yes, they are. And they would look very fine on you.

Balthazar: Yes, yes I believe they would. By the way, I am planning a journey with two other kings. We all need traveling boots. Could you make three pairs of traveling boots by next week, all size 12-B. *Aside to audience.* All kings wear size 12-B, you know.

Wife: Yes, certainly. We would be honored.

Balthazar: I will send a servant to collect my boots and pay for them. *Aside to audience.* Kings never carry money. They always wear size 12-B, and they never carry money. These are kingly facts. *To Husband and Wife.* Good day then, until next week. *King exits stage left.*

Wife: Heavens! Our luck has truly changed. Who will come for these, do you suppose?

Rabbit enters far stage left dressed as Santa Claus.

Rabbit: Ho, ho, ho.

Husband: Ho, ho, ho, Rabbit. You look wonderful. Why are you dressed as Santa Claus?

Rabbit: I really do look fine, don't I? Do you like my beard? I made it myself. I'm playing Santa Claus in the school play and I need some shiny black boots. Do you have any shiny black boots? *Pause.* Oh, look at these!

Wife: They would be perfect for you, Rabbit. And I think that they are just your size.

Rabbit picks up boots.

Rabbit: They are perfect. Shiny black leather, brass buckles. Yes! I'm going to be the best Santa ever!

Rabbit exits far stage left singing "Jingle Bells."

Husband: Ha, ha. Well dear, tonight we must find out who finished the shoes.

Wife: Yes indeed, and I know how to do it. We'll leave a bit of leather out, and hide behind the Christmas tree and wait. We'll find out who the secret shoemaker is if it takes all night.

Husband: Good idea. Here's the leather. *Reaches behind him.* Let's hide.

They hide behind the Christmas tree. Elf enters center stage as before.

Elf: They have gone to bed—time for me to work. Oh, only enough leather for one pair of shoes tonight. Well, I'll begin. Sew and sew, tap and tap, stitch and stitch, and that is that. All finished. Off I go!

Elf exits center stage as before. Husband and Wife come out of hiding.

Husband: An elf! My stars and garters! An elf made the shoes.

Wife: And did you see? That elf had no clothes on. Poor little shivery thing, all naked like that.

Husband: Well, we can fix that. Let's make the elf clothes to thank it for the work.

Wife: Right! First thing in the morning, we'll go and buy cloth and sew up a fine elf suit.

Husband: And I will make a pair of tiny elf boots.

Husband and Wife exit stage right. Sign appears and exits as before. It reads "December 24." Enter Husband and Wife stage left with cloth.

Husband: This won't take long with both of us working. What a fine way to spend Christmas Eve.

Wife: And tomorrow morning, on Christmas day, the elf will find these clothes waiting instead of pieces of leather to sew into shoes. It will be the finest-looking elf in the world!

Husband and Wife work on clothes.

Husband: Almost done!

Wife: There—finished. Put them on the counter and now we will hide behind the tree again and wait for the elf to come.

Husband and Wife put clothes on counter and hide behind Christmas tree. Elf enters center stage as before.

Elf: I hope that the shoemakers left more leather to stitch up. What is this? No leather, but look at this! A suit! A beautiful suit, and just my size. And boots! They must be for me. How splendid I will look!

Husband and Wife come out and hug elf.

Wife. Merry Christmas, helping elf, merry Christmas!

Elf: Thank you, thank you for my beautiful suit and boots. I will never be cold again.

Husband: It is we who must thank you for sewing our shoes and changing our luck.

Wife: Now you put on those clothes and get all warm and cozy while I fix us hot chocolate to drink.

Wife and elf exit stage right.

Husband: Merry Christmas, merry Christmas.

Husband exits stage right. Rabbit enters center stage with sign that reads "December 25."

Rabbit: Oh, would you like to know how the story ends? The elf put on its suit and was indeed the finest-looking elf in the world. The shoemakers' good luck continued, and they lived happily ever after. Little Red Riding Hood looked great in her shoes, and I was the best Santa ever. Everybody had a very merry Christmas and you must have a very merry Christmas too. The end, the end.

Little Red Riding Hood

Cast: Mother
Grandmother
Woodsman/Narrator
Little Red Riding Hood (LRRH)
Wolf

Props: Basket for Little Red Riding Hood, nightcap for Wolf (matches Grandmother's), wooden mallet for Woodsman.

Set: A forest center stage, LRRH's house stage left, Grandmother's house stage right.

Woodsman/Narrator steps forward at center stage.

Narrator: Once upon a time, a little girl lived with her mother on the edge of a forest. Her grandmother lived in a cottage on the other edge of the forest. *Narrator points at houses.* In the forest there lived a big, bad . . . wolf! That's right, a big bad wolf. Now this little girl was very, very vain. That means she thought about how pretty she was all the time. She looked in mirrors, and store windows, and ponds, and patted her hair and straightened her dress, and generally was just plain silly about her looks. Once she saw a woman who was wearing a red cape with a hood, and she fussed and begged until her mother made her a red cape with a hood. After that, she was called Little Red Riding Hood and no one even remembers her real name. Well, one day, her mother called her in from playing. This is what happened that day.

Narrator exits. Little Red Riding Hood enters followed by Mother stage left.
Mother: Little Red Riding Hood, I've just had word that your Granny is very ill and cannot get out of her bed. I want you to go through the forest to her cottage and take this basket of fruit, cakes, eggs, and honey to her.

LRRH: All right, Mommy. I'll wear my red cape and hood, and my green boots, and . . .

Mother: It doesn't matter what you wear dear. *Sighs.* Just get there quickly and safely. You are to follow the path straight to Granny's, and straight back. You are not to speak to anybody. And you are not to stray from the path.

LRRH: I won't. Granny will hardly know me in my new red riding hood. Why, the sight of me will probably make her completely well!

Mother: Oh dear! Well, when you get back we will have a talk about your cape, darling. Remember, no talking, no straying. Just there and back.

LRRH: Okay. Bye, Mommy.

LRRH starts to move to center stage while singing "Over the River and Through the Woods." Mother exits stage left.

LRRH: Ohh, look at that butterfly. And that one. And that one too. How beautiful. And look at those flowers. I'm sure Granny would like some of them.

Wolf appears from below stage level, just behind LRRH. He watches LRRH as she looks at flowers. He taps her on the shoulder.

LRRH: She turns to face Wolf. Oh! Help!

Wolf: Do not be alarmed, my dear. What are you doing all alone in the forest? Don't you know that these woods are full of wild beasts? And what are you carrying in that basket? I'm sure it must be much too heavy for a delicate child like you. And wherever did you get that stunning red cape? You look quite charming in it.

LRRH: Why, thank you, Mr. Wolf. Well, I'm on my way to my Granny's. She is not well, and I must take her this basket of food. It really isn't very heavy at all.

Wolf: What a brave little girl you are. But if your Granny is sick in bed, who will let you into the cottage?

LRRH: I tap on the door four times and say "Granny it's me," and she will tell me where the key is hidden.

Wolf: And is your Granny's house the one with the bluebird weathervane and the three potted geraniums in front?

LRRH: Yes, and it is ever such a long way from here.

Wolf: But you know, my dear, that this path is the very longest way to go to your Granny's. You want to go up that little hill there. *Gestures to rear of center stage.* And around the small pond at the bottom, then past the field of sunflowers, turn left at the spotted cow, and there you are! It is much shorter that way.

LRRH: Thank you, Mr. Wolf. Let's see, that's up the hill, around the pond, past the sunflowers, and left at the spotted cow. Got it. Goodbye, and thank you.

LRRH exits to back of stage center and down below stage level.

Wolf: That's right. Goodbye, goodbye, my dear. That's it. That's the shortcut. Heh, heh, heh. That little silly will be at least two hours getting to her Granny's house. I'll rush right over to Granny's house, gobble up the old one, and then wait for Little Red Riding Hood. She'll make a tasty afternoon snack. Heh, heh. *Goes off toward cottage, stage right.*

Wolf: Here we are. Red geraniums, bluebird weathervane, four taps. *Knocks four times.*

Granny: Yes. Who is it?

Wolf: Falsetto. It is I, Little Red Riding Hood. I've brought you a basket of goodies to make you well.

Granny: Are you sure you are Little Red Riding Hood? She doesn't know the rules of grammar very well, and she usually says "It is me," which is incorrect, you know.

Wolf: Oh, well. I have been working very hard at school, and my grammar has improved. I understand all about pronouns now, and say "It is I," which is correct. *To audience.* I think this Granny used to be a teacher.

Granny: That's lovely, dear. You'll find the key in the first geranium.

Wolf: Heh, heh. *Enters cottage.* Aha!

Granny: Why, you're not Little Red Riding Hood. You are the big bad Wolf. Help, help!

Wolf jumps at Granny and both disappear behind stage right. Wolf reappears stage right in Granny's cap.

Wolf: That Granny was certainly thin. Why, I just swallowed her whole. She's still wiggling around down there in my tummy. Be quiet in there, Granny. I'm going to have a nap while I wait for Little Red Riding Hood. *Lies down in bed and snores.*

LRRH enters stage center and moves toward stage right.

LRRH: Panting. I must have misunderstood that wolf's directions. That hill was very high, and the pond was a huge lake, and there was no spotted cow. At last. Here is Granny's house.

Wolf snores loudly.

LRRH: Heavens, Granny is snoring so loudly. I hope she will hear my knock. Oh, the door is open. *She enters the cottage.*

LRRH: Granny, Granny dear. She does not look well. Her skin is sort of gray. Granny?

Wolf: In falsetto. Is that you, Little Red Riding Hood?

LRRH: Yes, Granny. How are you feeling?

Wolf: I am so weak, my dear. Come a little closer to my bed so that we can talk.

LRRH: I have brought you some fruit, cake, honey, and eggs. Why, Granny, what very big eyes you have!

Wolf: All the better to see you with, my dear.

LRRH: Granny, what very large, hairy, pointy ears you have!

Wolf: All the better to hear you with, my dear.

LRRH: And Granny, what very long, sharp, white, huge, scary teeth you have!

Wolf: All the better to eat you with.

Wolf leaps up. LRRH screams and disappears below stage level, screaming continually. Wolf disappears barking at same spot. LRRH stops screaming, but does not reappear. Wolf reappears stage right.

Wolf: Where is she? She got away, but I will find her. Yoo hoo, little girl. Where are you?

Woodsman enters center stage and moves to stage right.

Woodsman: What is going on in there? I heard screaming. Are you all right, Granny?

Wolf: I'm just fine. You must have heard the television.

LRRH appears center stage and approaches Woodsman from behind.

LRRH: It was not the television. It was me screaming. That is not Granny. That is the big bad Wolf, and he tried to eat me up. And my grandmother is nowhere to be seen.

Woodsman: Hits wolf with mallet. Take that, Wolfie. Now, what have you done with Granny?

Granny: Very muffled from offstage. Help! Help!

Woodsman: What was that?

Granny: Still offstage. I said, help, help. Look in the wolf's mouth.

Woodsman: Open up, Wolf. *Looks in.* Why Granny is inside the wolf. Turn around, Wolf, and I will give you a smart smack between the shoulder blades.

Wolf turns around and Woodsman hits him on the back. Wolf coughs, his mouth below the stage level. Granny pops up from behind stage.

Granny: Well, I never. It was very warm and cozy inside that wolf. I'm feeling quite, well, tip-top. Like going to a spa! Thank you, Wolfie. Why don't you stay here in the cottage with me, and I will make you potato pancakes and jam tarts every day? Once you have eaten one of my jam tarts, you will never want to devour old grannies or little girls again.

Wolf: Okay. If it's all right with Mr. Woodsman.

Woodsman: Yes indeed, but if I hear one little cry from this cottage, it's the zoo for you, Mr. Wolf.

LRRH: Well, what about me? I got all hot and tired and dusty, and my red riding hood is all dirty, and . . .

All: Quiet!

Granny: Young lady, you are to go straight home, and you will try to be less vain. Looks aren't everything you know. And leave the basket.

LRRH: Oh. *Sniff.* Good-bye. I'll try. *Exits stage left.*

Granny: Come on, Wolfie. I have a lovely cushion for you by the fire. Let's see what is in this basket. *Granny and Wolf exit stage right.*

Woodsman: To audience. Little Red Riding Hood learned her lesson. She tried hard not to be so vain and learned all that she could about pronouns. She never talked to any wolves again, except for her grandmother's pet wolf. They became good friends. And that is the end of our play! The end! The end!

Maui: Two Legends

Maui Fishes Up the Island

Maui Ensnares the Sun

Cast: Narrator/Sun
Maui (foster child of gods)
Brother
Mother

Props: Flames, island.

Set: Waves, Island of Bolotu.

Narrator enters stage right and moves to center stage.

Narrator/Sun: We are going to show you the story of Maui. It is said that in the early days, the people who lived in the Pacific Islands did not have a barb for their spears. They did not have trap doors for their eel pots. It was Maui, the hero, who brought these things. It is said that in the beginning, when the gods lived on the island of Bolotu, the other islands were at the bottom of the sea. The legends say that it was Maui who brought them to the surface. Maui separated the earth from the sky and made the sun go slowly across the sky. Maui learned the secret of fire and brought that secret to the people. When he was born, Maui was small and misshapen, and his mother left him at the edge of the ocean. Maui was adopted by the gods of the ocean and was taught wisdom by his ancestors in the sky. When he grew up, Maui decided to return to the earth to find his family.

Narrator moves to stage left as Maui enters stage right and goes to center.

Narrator: Maui has three brothers. We will have only one brother in our play today. That brother will stand for all three.

Brother enters stage left from rear.

Narrator: Maui came upon his brothers playing a game called riti. They threw their spears against a rock to see whose spear would bounce the highest. They saw Maui and laughed at him. *Mime laughing.* Maui threw his spear against the rock so hard that the rock shattered into a million pieces. *Maui mimes this and brothers mime surprise.*

Maui: I am Maui, your brother. Come, I will show you how to carve a barb on your spear so that your fish will not fall off when you catch them. After that I will show you how to make a trap door for your eel pots so that when you catch eels the eels cannot escape.

Brother: Go away, Maui. We are going fishing. Here is our canoe. *Mime climbing into canoe at stage center.*

Maui: I will come too. *Mimes getting into canoe.*

Brother: Grumbles and grunts. Why does he insist on fishing with us? I wish he would go back to the sky to live.

They mime paddling. Maui stops and points stage left.

Maui: Stop! I will fish here. *Mimes throwing out line and pulling it in again and again, catching nothing.*

Brother: Why do you fish here, Maui? There are no fish here.

Maui: I will fish here. *Throws out line again.*

Brother: to audience He is a fool—and ugly too. Ha ha. He doesn't even know how to fish. Maui the hero! Ha! Oh, look!

Maui mimes feeling a strong tug and pulling in a heavy weight.

Maui: Help me, help me, brother.

Brother: No, no. The fish is so heavy that our canoe will tip over and sink if you try to reel in this giant fish. Let it go! Let go of the line! Let go of the line!

Maui: No! You must help me. You are my brother! Brother must help brother.

Brother: I will help.

The brother helps. A large land mass arises on stage left, lifted up and put in place by Narrator.

Maui: It is land! It is a fine new island!

Maui moves to stage right rear. Brother moves to stage left rear. Narrator goes to center stage.

133

Narrator: The new island broke into pieces. The biggest island was New Zealand. It is also called Te-ika-a-Maui—the fish that Maui caught. The other islands were Ata, Tonga, Samoa, and Fiji. Papa-langi, Vavau, and Maabai were also brought to the surface of the ocean by Maui. Time passed. Maui noticed that the days were very short. This was the reason why. Every day, the sun, Tama-nui-a-te-ra, came up in the east.

Sun enters far stage right.

Narrator: Then the sun raced across the sky.

Sun walks very quickly to stage left, makes a turn, and goes back to stage right. The head is lowered when not moving.

Narrator: It took about three hours for the sun to pass across the sky. Imagine, a day that was only three hours long. The people barely got their canoes in the water to fish when the sun set. They made tapa cloth and set it out in the sun to dry, and the sun would set. The tapa would be ruined before it dried out. Maui's mother went to him.

Maui moves from rear stage right to center stage front. Maui's mother enters stage right and moves to center stage.

Mother: Maui! The sun moves too quickly for us. There are not enough hours of sunlight for the people to complete their work. The fish are not caught and the fruits are not gathered. The tapa cloth does not dry. All because the day is too short. Can you help us, Maui? We are hungry!

Maui: I, Maui, will make the sun slow down!

Mother: How can this be done? The sun's heat is terrible. It will burn you.

Maui: You have seen what I can do. I raised great islands from the bottom of the ocean. Give me a net. Give me a club.

Mother mimes giving these to Maui. She goes to rear of center stage. From center stage Maui moves one step toward sun at stage right.

Maui: Mother, wait until the sun rises and then help me throw this net over the sun.

Sun: Rises up at stage right. It is day. I must run quickly to the other side of the world. Out of my way!

Maui: No, you don't! This net will stop you!

Maui and Mother mime throwing net at sun. Sun mimes being caught and struggles. Flames are thrown at Maui and his Mother. Maui beats at sun with an imaginary club and Mother continues to hang onto imaginary net.

Maui: There and there and there! *Match with blows.*

Sun: Ow! Ow! *Throws flames.* Why are you beating me? I am the mighty sun. What have I done?

Maui: I beat you because you refuse to go slowly across the sky. You must give the people many hours of sunlight to gather their food. They are hungry. You must give them sunlight to do their work. You must give them time to play, too. Slow down!

Sun: I don't care about the people. I will not slow down.

Maui: You will slow down. You will provide light for the people. As much as they need. *They struggle again. There are more blows and flames.*

Sun: Stop! Stop! You win. I promise I will go slowly across the sky and give the people many hours of light. They will be able to do all their work and play as well. Please let me go.

Fight stops. Maui and Mother mime removing net from sun.

Maui: There. You may go. Do not forget your promise.

Sun moves slowly across the stage, halting now and then to look back at Maui who uses a gesture to urge it forward. Sun reaches other side of stage and sinks.

Mother: Now there will be time to fish and dry tapa cloth.

Maui: Now there will be time to play.

Narrator: Moves to stage center. There were other things which Maui did for the people. There are many many stories about Maui and his children and grandchildren. Ask to hear them, listen well, and learn to tell those stories. Our play is over. The end.

All puppets move to center and bow.

135

The Three Little Pigs

Cast: Mother Pig
Pig 1 (wears glasses)
Pig 2 (wears bow tie)
Pig 3 (wears hair ribbon)
Man who sells straw (offstage)
Man who sells sticks (offstage)
Wolf

Props: House of straw; house of sticks; house of bricks; bundles of straw, sticks, and bricks; a fancy traveling hat and handbag for Mother; bow tie, hair ribbon, and glasses to distinguish pigs; green hair ribbon for Wolf's Girl Scout disguise.

Set: Trees on both sides of stage to suggest country setting.

Mother Pig enters stage right carrying sack and moves to center stage.

Mother: Children, children. Come here, darlings.

Pig 1 enters stage right.

Pig 1: Yes, Mom.

Pig 3 enters stage left.

Pig 3: Here we are, Mommy.

Pig 2 enters stage left.

Pig 2: We were playing Nintendo.

Mother: Yes, well, exactly. Life isn't all Nintendo and balloons, you know. I have decided to retire from the mothering business. So, you piglets are on your own. Here is $1.98 for each of you and some coupons. Let me know when you have made your fortunes, and I'll come for a visit. Goodbye. I'm off to Hawaii. Aloha, aloha, darlings, aloha. *exits stage right rear*

Pig 1: What? Well, hmm.

Pig 2: Bye, Mom! So, what's next?

Pig 1: Guess it's time to go seek my fortune.

Pig 2: Me too, I'm going to seek my fortune too. *Exits stage left.*

Pig 3: I think I will begin my search at the library. I'm going to look up books on housing, building materials career opportunities, and things like that. *Exits stage left.*

Pig 1: Gee, $1.98 is not very much money. What can I buy for $1.98?

Straw Man: offstage Straw! Straw for sale! Nice, dry, scratchy straw. Only $1.98 a bundle!

Pig 1: Mr. Straw Man, could a person, or a pig, make a house with that stuff?

Straw Man: Sure! It would be light and airy, and if you got hungry, you could chew on it a bit. It would make a great house.

Pig 1: Well I'll take a bundle then. Here's $1.98.

Straw Man: Thanks, pig. Good luck!

Pig 1: Let's see, it can't be that hard to make a house. I'll just put the straw down here and get to work.

Pig 1 works just below the edge of the stage. The tips of his ears show now and then. Grunts, panting, banging, sawing, and drilling noises are heard. Straw flies up in the air now and then, and at last a clumsy straw house rises up from behind the stage.

Pig 1: What a glorious edifice! Whew! I'm exhausted! I'm going to go inside and have a little nap.

Pig 1 goes into house. The sound of snoring comes from house. Wolf enters stage left singing "Over the River and Through the Woods." Stops when he sees house.

Wolf: Will you look at that? A straw house. *looks in window* There's a pig in there! *Snore from house.* It's asleep. Heh, heh, heh. *Tries window.* Window's too small. *Tries door.* Door's locked. Let's try a trick. Pigs are not very smart. *Knocks on door and says sweetly.* Piggy, oh little piggy, let me come in.

Pig 1: What? Who's out there? *Looks out window.* Oh no! It's the Big Bad Wolf. You want me to let you come in? Don't be silly, Wolfie. I'm not going to let you in—not by the hair on my chinny chin chin.

Wolf: Come on, piggy. Let me in.

Pig 1: No! Go away!

Wolf: Well then, I'll huff and I'll puff and I'll blow your house down. Here goes. *Blows lightly, but house stands.* Hmm. This house is sturdier than it looks. Boys and girls out there, would you help me blow this house down? You will? Great! On the count of three, then. One, two, three. *Blows and house falls down.*

Pig 1: Help, help. *Pig 1 runs away stage left, changes direction and exits stage right. Wolf wheels around confused.*

Wolf: Where is that pig? Is it out there? No? Oh fiddlesticks. I'll have to eat at McDonald's again.

Wolf exits. Pig 2 enters stage left.

Stick Man: Offstage. Sticks, sticks for sale. A million uses, all sizes. Sticks for sale. Only $1.98!

Pig 2: Looks stage right and behind. Hello, Stick Man. Say, could you build a house with those sticks?

Stick Man: Sure could! Easy as pie! Stick houses practically build themselves. And nothing can match a stick house for rustic charm.

Pig 2: Sold! Here's your $1.98. Let's see. I think I'll try a Dutch Colonial design.

Pig 2 Works just below edge of stage, tips of ears showing, sticks flying, and sounds of grunts, pants, hammering, sawing, drilling, etc. Stick house rises up into view.

Pig 2: Fantastic. Even if I do say so myself.

Wolf sings "Whistle While You Work" offstage.

Pig 2: Uh oh, it's the Big Bad Wolf. I finished my house just in time. Good thing I put a good strong lock on the door. *Goes into house.*

Wolf: Enters stage left whistling. What's this? Another silly-looking house. You know, this might just be another little piggy's house. *Creeps up and looks in window.* It is! It is a little piggy's house. *Sweetly.* Ah, little pig, oh little pig. Let me come in.

Pig 2: You must think I'm a silly pig, Big Bad Wolf. Well I'm not, and you are not coming in. Not by the hair of my chinny chin chin.

Wolf: Oh dear. Boys and girls, we are going to have to do that huffing and puffing stuff again. Will you help me blow this house down? OK? On the count of three. One, two, three, blow! *House does not fall down.* I guess this house is stronger than it looks. Let's try again, and this time, you adults out there, you blow too. Ready? One, two, three, Blow! *House falls down.*

Pig 2: Help, help, the Big Bad Wolf is after me! Help! Help!

Chase scene as before and Pig 2 disappears.

Wolf: Hey, where is that piggy? Where is it? These fat little piggies are faster than they look. And I missed my chance at another pig dinner. *Whiny.* It's McDonald's again for me.

Wolf exits stage right. Pig 3 enters stage left with a load of bricks.

Pig 3: Whew. These bricks are very heavy. But the library book on construction did say that bricks were the strongest building material one could use. And the bricks cost $1.98, just like the straw and sticks my brothers used. I wonder how they are doing. You know I really don't think you can build a strong and sturdy house out of straw or sticks. Oh well, if their houses don't work out they can come and live with me, and I can beat them at Scrabble every night. Let's see. I believe I'll build my house right here, with some windows facing east for the morning sun, and I'll put a garden over there.

Pig 3 puts bricks below stage level and begins working. She sings "The Eency Weency Spider." Sounds of some tapping. Pushes finished house up to stage level.

Pig 3: There we are. Now that is a house. Strong and sturdy and beautiful. I'm feeling a little hungry now with all that work. I think I'll just go inside and make some vegetable soup, and a carrot salad, and maybe an apple pudding for dessert.

Pig 3 enters house and can be seen puttering. Wolf enters stage left.

Wolf: I must be getting old. I just can't seem to catch piggies like I used to. Maybe it's my diet. Not enough leafy green vegetables or something. Hey, look at this. This might be another pig house. I don't know—it's a pretty sturdy-looking house. *Peers in window.* It is a pig house. Must be a smart piggy to have built such a fine house. I'm going to have to use trickery and guile this time. We wolves are very good at trickery and guile.

Wolf exits stage left, and returns with a green ribbon on his head, then knocks.

Wolf: Oh little pig, little pig, I'm a Girl Scout selling cookies. Please let me come in.

Pig 3: You are not a Girl Scout, and anyway I do not eat cookies. They are bad for your teeth. You are the Big Bad Wolf, and I'm not letting you in. Not by the hair of my chinny chin chin.

Wolf: What a smart piggy! I'll try something else.

Wolf exits stage left and returns with National Geographic *magazine in mouth. Drops it to speak.*

Wolf: Oh little pig, little pig, let me come in. I'm selling subscriptions to the *National Geographic* magazine.

Pig 3: I already have a subscription to the *National Geographic,* and you are the Big Bad Wolf. Wolfie, I'm not letting you in. Not by the hair of my chinny chin chin.

Wolf: Deep and gruff voice. Then I will huff and I'll puff and I'll blow your house down.

Pig 3: Go right ahead and try, Wolfie. This house is strong and sturdy.

Wolf: Okay, boys and girls. As you have heard, this is a very strong and sturdy house. I'm going to need all of your help. You grownups, you teachers and librarians, and moms and dads and grandmas and grandpas—even the babies. You all must help. Let's warm up a little bit. Whew, whew, whew, whew. *Little short breaths.* Good. Now we're ready. On the count of three. One, two, three, blow! *Everyone blows. Wolf pants as he talks.* Okay Now we're really ready. Again. One, two, three, blow. *Everyone blows. Wolf collapses over edge of stage, panting.* One last try then, everybody. One, two, three—blow! *Wolf falls backwards and disappears below stage level, then reappears using his mouth and/or paws to pull himself up to stage level, still panting.* Okay, now I'm really mad. This pig is just too smart. Well, I'll show her. I'm going to go up on the roof and down the chimney into the house. What do you think? Good idea! Cool, huh? Oh, well, I'm going to try it anyway.

Wolf climbs up roof with great difficulty, then slides off, slowly at first and then fast. He lands on ground crying.

Wolf: Oh, oh, nooooooo. Ow. Boo hoo hoo, boo hoo hoo!

Pig 3: Comes out of house. Wolfie, I tried to warn you but you wouldn't listen. Now look at you! You're a mess. Are you through trying to catch piggies?

Wolf: Sobs. Yes.

Pig 3: Do you promise that you will never try to catch piggies again?

Wolf: Never, never! I promise, I really, really do!

Pig 3: Good. Now get out of here. I never want to see you around here again! Get out! Shoo! Scoot! Scram!

Pig 3 makes shooing motions and Wolf, whimpering, exits stage left. Pig 1 and Pig 2 enter stage left.

Pig 1: Way to go, Sis. You sure got rid of the wolf.

Pig 2: And you built a swell house too!

Pig 3: It is quite splendid, isn't it? Would you like to live here with me?

Pig 1 and Pig 2: Yes! Sure!

Pig 2: And we'll do our own dishes and laundry.

Pig 1: I'll take out the garbage.

Pig 3: Fine! Now let's go in and have some lunch, and then we'll play a game of Scrabble. *exit Pigs 1 and 2 through house* Oh, this play is over. The end, the end, the end.

General Bibliography

Puppets and Puppetry

Champlin, Connie. *Puppetry and Creative Dramatics in Storytelling.* Phoenix: Oryx, 1991.

Coad, Luman, and Arlyn Coad. *Producing for the Puppet Theater.* North Vancouver, B.C.: Charlemagne Press, 1987.

Currell, David. *Learning with Puppets.* Boston: Plays, Inc., 1990.

Engler, Larry. *Making Puppets Come Alive: A Method of Learning and Teaching Hand Puppetry.* New York: Taplinger, 1973.

Feller, Ron. *Paper Masks and Puppets for Stories, Songs, and Plays.* Seattle: Arts Factory, 1985.

Fijan, Carol, and Frank Ballard. *Directing Puppet Theatre Step by Step.* San Jose: Resource Publications, 1989.

Frazier, Nancy, and Nancy Renfro. *Imagination: At Play with Puppets and Creative Drama.* Austin, Tex: N. Renfro Studios, 1987.

Frog Print Theater. *The One-Person Puppet Show.* Ontario, Canada: Ontario Puppetry Association, 1981.

Jenkins, Peggy Davison. *The Magic of Puppetry: A Guide for Those Working with Young Children.* Englewood Cliffs, N.J.: Prentice-Hall, 1980.

Magon, Jero. *Staging the Puppet Show.* North Vancouver, B.C.: Charlemagne Press, 1989.

Marks, Burton, and Rita Marks. *Puppet Plays and Puppet-Making: The Plays, the Puppets, the Production.* Boston: Plays, Inc., 1985.

Painter, William. *Musical Story Hours: Using Music with Storytelling and Puppetry.* Hamden, Conn.: Library Professional Publications, 1989.

Rountree, Barbara. *Creative Teaching with Puppets: Resources for Six Integrated Units.* University, Ala.: Learning Line, Inc., 1981.

Schramm, Toni A. *Puppet Plays: From Workshop to Performance.* Englewood, Colo.: Teacher Ideas Press, 1993.

Sierra, Judy. *Fantastic Theater: Puppets and Plays for Young Performers and Young Audiences.* New York: H. W. Wilson, 1991.

Sierra, Judy, and Robert Kaminski. *Multicultural Folktales: Stories to Tell Young Children.* Phoenix: Oryx, 1991.

Sims, Judy, and Beverly Armstrong. *Puppets for Dreaming and Scheming: A Puppet Source Book.* Walnut Creek, Calif.: Learning Works, 1988.

Warren, Jean, and Gary Mohrman. *Everyday Patterns.* Everett, Wash.: Warren Publishing House, 1990.

Wright, Denise Anton. *One-Person Puppet Plays.* Englewood, Colo.: Teacher Ideas Press, 1990.

Children's Books on Puppets and Puppetry

Hunt, Tamara, and Nancy Renfro. *Celebrate! Holidays, Puppets and Creative Drama.* Austin, Tex.: N. Renfro Studios, 1987.

Hunt, Tamara, and Nancy Renfro. *Pocketful of Puppets: Never Pick a Python for a Pet and Other Animal Poems.* Austin, Tex.: N. Renfro Studios, 1984.

Lasky, Kathryn, and Christopher Knight. *Puppeteer.* New York: Macmillan, 1985.

Lynch-Watson, Janet. *The Shadow Puppet Book.* New York: Sterling, 1980.

Renfro, Nancy. *Puppet Shows Made Easy!* Austin, Tex: Renfro, n.d.

Supraner, Robyn. *Plenty of Puppets to Make.* Mahwah, N.J.: Troll, 1981.

Warren, Jean, and Cora L. Walker. *1, 2, 3 Puppets: Simple Puppets to Make for Working with Young Children.* Everett, Wash.: Warren Publishing House, 1989.

Wood, Geraldine. *Jim Henson: From Puppets to Muppets.* Minneapolis: Dillon, 1987.

Wright, Lynda. *Puppets.* London and New York: Watts, 1989.

Young, Ed, and Hilary Beckett. *The Rooster's*

Horns: A Chinese Puppet Play to Make and Perform. New York: Collins & World, 1978.

Storytelling

Bauer, Caroline Feller. *Handbook for Storytellers.* Chicago: American Library Association, 1977.

Bauer, Caroline Feller. *Read for the Fun of It: Active Programming with Books for Children.* New York: H. W. Wilson, 1992.

MacDonald, Margaret Read. *Finding, Learning, Performing, and Using Folktales, Including Twelve Tellable Tales.* Little Rock: August House, Inc., 1993.

Twenty Tellable Tales. New York: H. W. Wilson, 1986.

Pellowski, Anne: *The Story Vine: A Source Book of Unusual and Easy to Tell Stories from Around the World.* New York: Macmillan, 1984.

Schimmel, Nancy. *Just Enough to Make a Story: A Sourcebook for Storytelling* 2d ed. Berkeley: Sisters' Choice Press, 1982.

Sierra, Judy, and Robert Kaminski. *Twice upon a Time: Stories to Tell, Retell, Act Out and Write About.* New York: H. W. Wilson, 1989.

Bibliographies and Other Useful Books

Albyn, Carole Lisa, and Lois Sinaiko Webb. *The Multicultural Cookbook for Students.* Phoenix: Oryx, 1993.

Austin, Mary C., and Esther Jenkins. *Promoting World Understanding Through Literature, K–8.* Englewood, Colo.: Libraries Unlimited, 1983.

Best Books for Children. New York: Bowker, 1990.

Hayden, Carla D., ed. *Venture into Cultures: A Resource Book of Multicultural Materials and Programs.* Chicago: American Library Association, 1992.

Heath, Alan. *Windows on the World: Multicultural Festivals for Schools and Libraries.* Metuchen, N.J.: Scarecrow Press, 1991.

Ireland, Norma Olin, and Joseph W. Sprug. *Index to Fairy Tales.* All editions and supplements. Lanham, Md., Scarecrow Press, 1973, 1979, 1989, 1994.

Lee, Lauren K. *Elementary School Library Collection: A Guide to Books and Other Media:*

Phases 1-2-3. Williamsport, Pa.: Brodart Co., 1996.

Lima, Carolyn W., and John A. Lima. *A to Zoo: Subject Access to Children's Picture Books.* New York: Bowker, 1993.

Miller-Lachman, Lyn. *Our Family, Our Friends, Our World: An Annotated Guide to Significant Multicultural Books for Children and Teenagers.* New York: Bowker, 1990.

Peterson, Carolyn Sue, and Benny Hall. *Story Programs: A Source Book of Materials.* Metuchen, N.J.: Scarecrow Press, 1980.

Pilger, Mary Anne. *Multicultural Projects Index: Things to Make and Do to Celebrate Festivals, Cultures, and Holidays Around the World.* Englewood, Colo.: Libraries Unlimited, 1991.

Sinclair, Patti K. *E for Environment: An Annotated Bibliography of Children's Books with Environmental Themes.* New Providence, N.J.: R. R. Bowker, 1992.

Video

Henson, Jim. *The World of Puppetry.* 6 Vols. Chicago: Films Incorporated, 1989.

TeleJapan USA and Pacific Mountain Network. *Puppeteer's Apprentice.* United States: Pacific Mountain Network, 1988.

Journals

UNIMA Pupperty Journal. A Propos. Puppeteers of America.

Organizations

Puppeteers of America, 5 Cricklewood Path, Pasadena, CA 91107-1002. Telephone: 818-797-5748. Puppeteers of America publishes an annual directory. There are 34 local guilds affiliated with this national group. If you call or write, Chairperson Gayle G. Schluter will give you the location of the guild closest to you.

UNIMA (American Center of the Union Internationale de la Marionette), c/o Allelu Kurten, Browning Road, Hyde Park, NY 12538 Telephone: 914-266-5953.

Sound Effects

The Complete Sound Effects Library (compact disc). New York: Sony Music Entertainment Inc., 1992.

About the Author

JEAN POLLOCK is a graduate of the University of Victoria, Victoria, B.C. She earned her M.L.S. from the University of California at Los Angeles. She has been a children's librarian in Los Angeles Public Library, The Oakland Public Library, and currently in the King County Library System of Seattle, Washington. In addition to children's services, she has been active in library literacy programs and family literacy programs.